Gathered Before the Lord

The Shape of Today's Liturgy

Gathered

Before

the Lord

The Shape of Today's Liturgy

by Joseph Lange

Christian Classics, Inc.

P.O. Box 30 • Westminster, MD 21157

First published 1990

© 1990 by Joseph Lange

Library of Congress Catalog Number: 90-081545

ISBN: 0-87061-174-7

Printed in the United States of America

For John Conmy, O.S.F.S.

Acknowledgments

Grateful acknowledgment is made to *Church World* and its editor, Henry Gosselin. Much of this material appeared in *Church World,* the diocesan paper of Portland, Maine. All of it has been completely reworked from a different point of view.

Thanks, too, to Bvonne Rossetti, who typed the manuscript.

Contents

Preface

On the west side of town there was some undeveloped land, part meadow, part woodland. A couple of bird-watchers searched through their binoculars and came away congratulating themselves for having seen twenty-three different species. Some children found it a delightful place for hide-and-seek. An artist saw it as forms and colors and textures. A developer saw it as things to be moved and rearranged—in his mind's eye he envisioned a housing development. A naturalist walked through it discovering little holes, homes for little creatures; he saw lots of other things, too, which everybody else missed.

What we see, perceive, experience, depends on our perspective. What one perspective reveals, another ignores. The following reflections stem from a perspective that regards the parish *as a community that grows saints*. From that perspective the weekly liturgy is a weekly meeting of the community to further the process of growing saints. There are, to be sure, other ways of looking at liturgy, but this is mine: once a week we get together, and something important should come of that.

This is a very personal book. Its deepest source is personal, but it is also pastoral. It is personal because it is the temporary result of forty years of struggling with the experience of being a Christian, a Catholic, and a priest. It is pastoral because it is about what we are doing as Church to foster the growth of our people into a holy people whose business it is to bring about the reign of God.

The primary focus of this book is our Catholic Eucharistic liturgy or, as I prefer to call it, our weekly gathering. I will be looking at what we are doing and asking why. Each question raises other issues. Over the years I have tried to understand what I am doing as a leader in the Church and a leader of liturgy. It hardly needs to be said that everything has changed and many firmly held opinions, attitudes, convictions and practices have been challenged.

I am uneasy about one aspect of these reflections. Here and there I take some time to digress about things like cultural influences and prayer, not to try to treat these things exhaustively, but to show their influence on the matter at hand. Nor am I so silly as to believe that my readers are unacquainted with these things. I am silly about other things, but not this. Sometimes, as with prayer, I describe it so that we will have a common understanding.

I have rarely run into anyone who understands how radically things have changed, how radically different the Vatican II liturgy is from what preceded it. In fact, in spite of this transformation, the liturgy in practice remains regrettably traditional, except that the language is English.

The bishops of the Council seemed to have had high hopes for the reform they were initiating. Almost everybody has heard their words: the Eucharistic liturgy is "the summit toward which the activity of the Church is directed; at the same time it is the fount from which all the Church's power flows."

When these words first appeared, a friend of mine said, "Either this is a case of shooting elephants with water pistols, or we have a lot to learn about liturgy." In the seventies a priest told me, "We counted on the new liturgy to form community and to do all sorts of good things. It hasn't worked." Another priest told me the same thing last year.

The bishops really did have high hopes for the liturgical reform. So did many of us who began to come of age in the sixties. Those hopes have rarely been fulfilled. What's going on? Why is there a problem?

I don't think we have to look far for an answer. Our weekly liturgies are gatherings of the Church, and so what we do in our liturgies depends on what we understand by *Church*. What are we for as *Church*? How are we *Church*? What sorts of things are we concerned about as *Church*? What sorts of things do we do as *Church*?

At the Council the bishops undertook reform not only of the liturgy but of our outlook on Church. The "summit and source" can reach the high hopes only if the rest is being taken into account.

Liturgists, whether professional or local, are often constrained to "bring off" this week's liturgy. Liturgical literature abounds with books on "how to do it," with books on how to understand the seasons and how to get the most out of the Sacramentary.

This is not one of those kinds of books. For that reason I am going to roam over other fields. Again, that is why this book is personal *and* pastoral. The people who gather for liturgy are the heart of the matter, and they are by and large ill prepared to make anything happen. Where are they coming from? What is their understanding of what they are about?

The narrowness of most of the liturgical concerns I have encountered is the reason for this book, and for these reflections. I have few pretensions about the extent to which I can adequately deal with all the issues I raise. Nevertheless, I present what I have, knowing that the struggle is far from complete.

It will take generations for us to come to terms with what Vatican II began. The thoughts, questions, conclusions that follow are meant to be starting points, not endings. They are the simple reflections of a rather ordinary person who is severely limited by all the social, cultural, and personal strictures that affect us all.

Part One

Some Background

The radical newness of our current attempts at liturgy might be more easily grasped if we first take a look at what we were doing before the second Vatican Council. What we had then was "the Holy Sacrifice of the Mass." It was the Latin rite of the Roman Catholic Church, uniform throughout the world only since the Council of Trent in the sixteenth century. Prior to that, different areas had their own rites. Trent imposed uniformity, and it took about seventy-five years for that to be achieved.

The celebrant of the Holy Sacrifice of the Mass was the priest. It was expected that he would prepare himself to "say" Mass. Often there was a kneeler in the sacristy with prayers from the Missal for "prayers before Mass." There were prayers and ritual for putting on each vestment. The priest and the altar boy would make their way into the sanctuary. The people would rise as the priest came in and then kneel for the "prayers at the foot of the altar." The sanctuary was set off by an altar rail because this was the holy space where the Holy Sacrifice of the Mass would take place. Only special people (all male) were allowed in that holy space.

After the prayers at the foot of the altar the priest would ascend to the altar and, with his back to the people, read the prayers and the scripture reading in Latin, the book being changed to the gospel side by the altar boy. He might then preach, though there was no obligation to do so, nor was there any obligation to deal with the scripture of the day.

In those days we didn't consider the scriptures to be very important. We were obliged to attend Mass on Sundays on pain of mortal sin, and when the question came up "How much can you miss without committing a mortal sin?" the answer was: "You must be present from the offertory to the priest's communion." It really was not important to be present for the scripture readings. The priest, of course, was the central figure. He alone was authorized and empowered to consecrate the bread and wine.

After the Gospel, then, the priest would begin the offertory. We sat through this. He would uncover the
chalice and paten. The altar boy would get ready with
the cruets of water and wine, and the priest with
prayers and signs of the cross would offer the bread
and wine to God. Then came the canon beginning
with the preface, to which we responded *"Sanctus,
sanctus, sanctus . . . "* Then all knelt down.

When the priest came to the *Hanc igitur,* the server
would ring bells to alert us that the consecration was
coming. After the *Hoc est enim Corpus meum,* the
priest would genuflect, raise the host with the ringing
of the bells, and genuflect again. A similar procedure
followed for the consecration of the wine. At the
"elevations" we would strike our breasts and say
something to ourselves like "My Lord and my God."

The next important moment was communion. We
only had to stay until the priest's communion to avoid
mortal sin, but we were encouraged to "receive."
When we did, we received only on our tongue and
were careful not to chew. Only the priest was allowed
to touch the host with his fingers. As a matter of fact,
he touched it only with his thumb and index fingers,

3

which he kept pressed together from the consecration till after communion, when he washed them.

We were allowed to make our first holy communion when we knew that the host was really the body of Christ. This was the meaning of communion: Christ was our food; he became really present in us.

There were, of course, variations of Masses, the unbloody sacrifice of the cross. There were High Masses and Solemn High Masses. There were dialogue Masses. Whatever, we were encouraged to use a missal and follow along with *what the priest was doing*.

For most there was something very special about going to Mass. There was a sense of the sacred, of God's presence. That was good. That was very good.

On the other hand, this Latin rite communicated, taught, a number of other things. Since only the priest said the Mass, we learned that we did not. We attended *his* Mass. Since bells were rung and breasts were struck only to announce the Real Presence, we never learned to look for God's presence in the assembly or in his word. Perhaps the hardest thing to grasp is that the sense of the sacred was so clearly encountered in the unusual (Latin, sacred space, tabernacle, sacred priest, sacred music) that we were diverted from looking for God in the ordinary. As we learned to find God in the Mass, we learned to look for the sacred only in church, through sacred people, from the consecration to communion, in the tabernacle.

At the risk of belaboring the obvious, our image of Church was predominantly institutional and hierarchical. Because we imaged Church as institutional, it was something we belonged to. That feels right: we belong to institutions. Because it was hierarchical, we felt that all power and authority resided in the hierarchy.

This shaped our liturgical piety. What counted was what the hierarchy did—in this case, the priest. We attended the priest's Mass: "May the Lord accept this sacrifice from *your* hands . . . " It didn't matter what we did while the priest said Mass as long as we were present. We could read from our missals or prayer books, or pray the rosary, or anything. What really counted was the Eucharist, the consecration and the priest's communion.

Another dimension of that piety was that the church was God's house and we were to be quiet in God's house. The church was dominated by the presence of Christ in the tabernacle. We genuflected to the tabernacle when entering and leaving.

The silence of our piety meant that we came to church to be alone in our prayers. We were quiet so as not to disturb someone else at prayer and so that we could get down to the business of saying our own prayers. The piety was about saving *my* soul, a God-me piety. Church was an institution *I* belonged to.

This brief description, with obvious drawbacks, was our experience of the Holy Sacrifice of the Mass. The new liturgy is communitarian: the people celebrate, the priest presides. The word of God has been restored. The image of Church as predominantly institutional and hierarchical has been abandoned for an image of a pilgrim people, a community of disciples of Jesus whose business it is to bring about the reign of God.

When the bishops declared that the Eucharistic liturgy is "the summit toward which the activity of the Church is directed," they did not mean that there are not other moments in which the compassion of Christ shows brilliantly or other moments in which the truth of Christ or the peace of Christ are felt. They saw the faithful coming together weekly to praise God, to be nourished by the word of God, to celebrate the paschal mystery, and to renew the covenant in the breaking of the bread and the sharing of the cup. They wrote:

> The liturgy in its turn moves the faithful, filled with the "paschal sacraments," to be "one in holiness"; it prays that "they may hold fast in their lives to what they have grasped by their faith"; the renewal in the Eucharist of the covenant between the Lord and his people draws the faithful into the compelling love of Christ and sets them on fire.

The bishops readily acknowledge that the liturgy is not everything. They are very clear that many things must happen if the new liturgy is to work, if it is to set us "on fire." (It's an astounding idea: the bishops expect us to be set "on fire" by the liturgy.)

The force that makes the weekly gathering the "summit" is that it symbolizes and expresses the coming *together* of a people who are disciples of Jesus, who want to deepen their relationship with God and with each other by coming *together* before him, by listening and responding *together* to his word, by remembering *together*, by renewing *together* the covenant in his body and blood.

The bishops indicated a number of things that must happen if the new liturgies are to work. They were very clear about the absolute requirement that those who take part in the liturgies must be people of prayer. People who are disciples of Jesus must be people of prayer. They quote Paul, who says "Pray always."

The sacramental rites are structures within which God's people gather to "stand in his presence." If we come only to attend, if we do not come to meet God, then we have empty religion. We have made the mistake of eating the husk and throwing away the grain. We mistake the structure for the encounter.

So, another thing the bishops saw as essential is the instruction of the clergy—first, that they may see to the instruction of the faithful in prayer; secondly, that they may see to it that their people are adequately prepared; and, thirdly, that they may preside thoroughly knowing and understanding what they are about.

Another thing the bishops insisted was necessary is a love of scripture: since "it is from the scripture that actions derive their meaning . . . it is essential to promote that warm and living love for scripture to which the venerable tradition of both Eastern and Western rites give testimony."

What the bishops are saying so clearly is that rituals don't work just because they are official. The Eucharistic liturgy is the work of people who are already disciples, already people of prayer, already in love with the scripture, already a people of the covenant.

Anyone who has tried to paint a house knows that preparing the surface is the most important and the most time-consuming part of the process. Liturgical reform is like that. We don't get liturgical reform simply by changing the ritual. There are no shortcuts. Christian liturgies are the rituals of *Christians* gathered together before God. If the major part of our effort in renewal is not about conversion and prayer, then re-forming the rituals is futile.

Another preliminary notion is the idea of sacrament. I don't like the word *sacrament*. It is part of our Catholic heritage, part of Catholic language, but is a specialized word, a technical word. It creates feelings of something religious as opposed to something ordinary. The word *sacrament* is not part of ordinary language about ordinary things. When I speak of the sacrament of anointing the sick, it feels like I'm in a different world from sending a get-well card or calling or visiting. For so many of us, there is the world of religion and the rest of our lives. Some would call it the secular and the sacred. The world of religion is the world of hymns, or prayers and devotions. Everything else is unrelated except for rules, especially about sexuality.

A woman once shared with a group of us that only recently had she come to see that being a Christian had to do with all of her life. She said, "I thought that religion had to do with saying prayers and going to church. I thought that the rest was just being neighborly."

We don't need the word *sacrament,* but we need the idea. The word means "make holy." It is a statement of belief about reality. It means that *there is no distinction between the secular and the sacred.* We believe that we can discover God in and through the material world and in all that is human. If we make something special of our religious rites and rituals, of symbols and signs, of words and gestures, of bread and wine, of water and salt and oil, it is only so that we may discover God in sunsets and falling leaves, too, in the smile of a friend, in a baby we hold close to our heart, in the dishes we wash, in the person we are selling something to, in the welcome we give one another, in the hug we give—yes, and even in the image that looks back at us from a mirror.

If we are to find God when we gather as Church, then we must first be able to find the divine life in our everydayness, close to home. A young lady once told me that she was sitting by a window reading the Bible one day. As she looked out the window and saw the tree in her very small front yard, the thought occurred to her, "My Father made that tree." She said, "I went outside and looked around, and the whole world seemed different. I kept saying to myself things like 'My Father made each blade of grass here. My Father made that sparrow . . . and the blue sky . . . and the clouds'."

A man once told me that he made a Cursillo and, for the first time in his life, really opened his heart to the presence and love of Christ. He owned a factory. He said he went back to work on Monday and, instead of going to his office, went to the floor of the factory and walked among the people working there. He said to me, "For the first time I saw people, not just employees. I began to visit everyday. I asked people their names and how long they had worked there. I asked about their families. In the summer I gave a picnic for them and their families." He went on, "Everything changed. People began to enjoy working in my factory. Production went up. I feel God's presence now when I go there. I feel as though I'm helping a little bit to bring about God's kingdom where I am."

The idea of sacrament is that all of life is holy, that we find God in and through the material, in and through all that is human. For some of us it means rediscovering awe and wonder; and that means paying attention, being present to whoever or whatever is simply there in front of us. We were that way once as little children before we were trained to do something "useful."

I know a man, a truck driver, who had a wonderful experience, repeated many times since. When his wife came home from the hospital with their first baby, he took it in his big hands and just looked at it for two hours. He was overcome with wonder and awe. He said he had never felt so close to God.

I know another man who has two big dogs. He told me that every evening when he comes home from work, those dogs come bounding down the driveway to meet him as he gets out of the car. They bark and jump around and wag their tails. He asked me, "Why don't any of the human members of my family make me feel so welcome?"

Liturgies, sacramental rites, sum up and express what we are about all the time, discovering God in the material and the human. *God is only as present in our liturgies as he is anywhere else in our experience.* People who do not discover God at the wedding reception will not discover God at the wedding Mass. People who do not discover God in their Bibles will not discover God in the Liturgy of the Word.

13

To bring this part of these reflections to a close, here are a few thoughts about the community dimension of our liturgy. Liturgy, in fact, is about a community at worship. Without a real coming together as community to stand before the Lord together, what is supposed to happen just does not happen. A conversion to community is an essential part of being a disciple of Jesus.

At the same time that Jesus promised us the Spirit, he prayed that we might be one even as he and the Father are one. And (please don't miss this) he prayed that this unity in him would be the sign to the world that he had been sent from the Father.

Jesus was the sign, the sacrament, of the Father: "He who sees me sees the Father." We, together, united in Christ are the sign, the sacrament of Christ. He is the vine, we are the branches. He is the head, we are the body. We now are the Christ presence, the messianic presence in the world. "Love one another as I have loved you."

This is why the bishops said that our weekly gathering could be the source and the highest expression of our Christian life. All week long we have been scattered. Now we come together. We are assembled in one place. What we are about *together* can be seen by what we do and how we do it. This is the idea of sacrament. What we do and how we do it reveals Christ.

We come *together,* Christians, disciples of Jesus, joined to him and to each other in our baptism, filled with his Spirit, people of prayer, eager for his life-giving word, eager to be together, eager to come together before him as his people, to listen and respond from our hearts, to offer praise and thanksgiving, to renew the covenant that makes us one in his body and blood.

In 1978, *Environment and Art in Catholic Worship* was published by the U.S. Bishops' Committee on the Liturgy. Here is how they said it:

> To speak of environmental and artistic requirements in Catholic worship, we have to begin with our-selves—we who are the Church, the baptized, the initiated.
>
> Among the symbols with which liturgy deals, none is more important than this assembly of believers. It is common to use the same name to speak of the building in which those persons worship, but that

15

> use is misleading. In the words of ancient Chris-
> tians, the building used for worship is called *domus
> ecclesiae,* the house of the Church.
>
> The most powerful experience of the sacred is found
> in the celebration and the persons celebrating, that
> is, it is found in the action of the assembly: the
> living words, the living gestures, the living sacri-
> fice, the living meal.

Do you understand how enormous this change of perspective is? Reread the quotation. The most important symbol is the assembly itself. "The most powerful experience of the sacred . . . is found in the action
of the assembly." There is a completely different reality here from when we "went to church" to be present at "the priest's Mass," when the most powerful
experience of the sacred came as the bells rang to sig-
nal the consecration.

The conversion to community is, in part, from going
to church to *being Church,* from attending the priest's
Mass to celebrating together with the priest presiding.

Let me continue the contrast between pre- and post-
Council liturgical piety. If we see the weekly gathering as the priest's Mass, then what we do does not
matter. If we are asked to sing or listen or respond, it
just does not seem important whether we do it or not.

What counts is what Father does. On the other hand, if *we* are the Church and this assembly is *our* gathering before the Lord, then everything *we do together* is what makes the assembly work. What's difficult, if we have never come together this way, if we have never experienced the power of coming together this way, then we do not even know that anything is missing.

Finally, solutions to problems depend on correctly identifying the problems. Lack of attendance or participation can be blamed on apathy or the lack of gifted liturgical ministers. If that is the case, then we look for leaders who can generate enthusiasm, liturgies that are exciting, musical leaders who are gifted. We create performances, and those performances "come off" only when we have good leaders. I truly believe that most of the criticism of such performances is justified.

On the other hand, if the problem of participation is the lack of real conversion to Jesus, if the reason we don't sing is that we don't have a song in our hearts, we don't need performers: we need *conversion*. Furthermore, even if we have an assembly of the converted, if they perceive that Mass is what the priest

17

does, then there doesn't seem to be any worthwhile reason for their doing anything. What is needed is conversion to *community in Christ*. Then we have sacrament, the liturgy of the assembled community. We have gone beyond performance to the ministry of the worshipping community.

Part Two
The People Who Celebrate

The recent Notre Dame study on the parish reported that over ninety percent of pastors are dissatisfied with their parish councils. That is hardly surprising. Most of the people elected to parish councils have little, or even a wrong, understanding of Church and little or no understanding of what they are about as a council.

Some years ago, I sat in on a parish liturgy committee meeting preparing for Lent. The religious education coordinator was giving them instructions: "Pick a different symbol (like salt, water, etc.) for each Sunday, then find scripture to go with the symbol." Unbelievable.

My point is that we can't get what we're supposed to get unless the people involved know what they are doing. The bishops certainly saw that, since they indicated that the people had to be prepared or the reform wouldn't work. My own experience is that this dimension of preparation is the most consistently ignored activity of people involved with liturgy.

What are we supposed to be like, we who gather each week in our church buildings? Are we, in fact, anywhere closer to what we are supposed to be? Earlier I described us as *eager* to celebrate, *eager* to sing, and so forth. I knew it rang false, that we rarely encounter such a gathering, but I was describing an ideal. We gather as Christians, as initiated disciples of Christ.

Not many of us Catholics call ourselves Christians. It's not something we were brought up to do. Some people do, of course, and we feel a little uncomfortable about them. They must have learned it through contact with evangelical Christians. It is enough for us to identify ourselves as Catholic.

Why are we uncomfortable with identifying ourselves as Christians? Do we associate "Christian" with "non-Catholic"? Does being Christian mean being associated with people connected with TV evangelism? Is it related to the fact that, in the past, Catholic culture identified more with the Church than with Christ *(The*

Church teaches . . .)? Aren't we more shaped by our culture than by Christ?

Does identifying ourselves as Christians seem to demand more of us than simply being Catholic? I think it does. I think it has to do with our resistance. We can call ourselves Catholic without feeling a lot of pressure; we are claiming membership in a Church. But a Church is impersonal. It is vague and undemanding. It is like other volunteer organizations. I don't need to know a whole lot about it and I don't have to agree with all that it is about. I fit its requirements into my schedule, my way of thinking, my values. It is commonplace among Church professionals that Church obligations are the first to go when it comes to competing activities. People who wouldn't dream of missing a bowling night or a Weight Watchers meeting have all sorts of excuses for missing parish commitments.

On the other hand, if we call ourselves Christians, then somehow, however vaguely, there is a sense of relatedness to God in Christ, a relatedness that makes demands far beyond relatedness to a Church.

21

Those who belong to a Church fit the Church into their lives. Those who belong to Christ fit their lives into God—"May *your* will be done, may *your* kingdom come."

Being a Christian strikes at the roots of self-sufficiency, self-centeredness, autonomy. "Whoever saves his life will lose it."

To be a Christian is to be a disciple of Christ. To be a disciple is to be one who *wants* to learn, one who comes to Christ to learn how to live. A disciple is not a student of academic learning, but a student of living. In earlier times a disciple would live with the master, learning a new way of life. In the beginning, Christianity was known as "The Way," a way of life.

Are you a Catholic? "Yes, I go to church on Sundays and most holy days, and I try to keep the commandments."

Are you a Christian? Do you seek first the reign of God and his justice? Do you love God with all your heart and soul and strength and mind? Do you read, re-read, ponder and struggle with the Gospels? Do you want—really want—to know and follow the teachings of Jesus?

We are, of course, talking about conversion; but before we get to that rather slippery idea, I want to explore some other dimensions of who we are, we who gather in church each week.

We are more American and Catholic than we are Christians. We have absorbed cultural values and behaviors as everyone else does because they are the more or less common stock of knowledge and that's what "everybody else does." Through the forties, for example, divorce was rare among Catholics in America—but it was also rare among the rest of Americans. Once American culture allowed easy divorce, so did American Catholics. There is no appreciable difference in the divorce rate among Catholics today and American society at large.

The predominant American values are comfort, convenience, mobility, privacy, autonomy, and greed. I think it is rather interesting, as someone pointed out, that all these values come together in a single symbol: the car. (American culture has its symbols, too.) It's no wonder that having a car in America is such an

23

important experience. It would be no trouble at all to write a few thousand words on each of these American values, but it hardly seems necessary. These values produce a way of life that is lived all around us. It is us. Not to live out of these values is to be odd, and who wants to be odd? Who wants to even think about it?

Later on I want to develop the idea of a community at worship. For now I want to note that every one of these American values is, in its own way, an obstacle to community, and perhaps none more so than autonomy or individualism. The conversion to community is by far the most difficult for Americans to grasp and, even if understood and accepted, the most difficult to bring about.

The highly prized, the most pervasive American quality is individualism. In America I have a right to go where I want, say what I please, do my own thing. There is a string in the heart of each one of us that resounds with Frank Sinatra's "I did it my way." There is little sense of the common good or the common life. Any thought of belonging to a group creates fears of losing my independence. I may be part of a group of like-minded people, but on my terms.

There is a place in American society for religion, but it is a very limited place. One is allowed to fit some religious activities into one's life, but not too many. Religious people are more or less tolerated, more tolerated if their religiosity allows them to be violent, greedy, selfish, self-sufficient. And like the rest of us, the trick, once again, is to fit religion into one's life in a way that doesn't make one different.

American culture, too, is still patriarchal. Tremors of feminism have shaken the massive citadel of patriarchy. Cracks are spreading through the foundations like spider webs. The end is coming, but the war has only just begun. It is still easier for women to be serious about discipleship because "they need it," "they like that sort of thing," and so on. Interestingly, this is a fairly recent phenomenon. In earlier cultures only men were considered fit for religion.

Western man, American man, has become soft. There is plenty of the macho, of the pseudo strength, of the violence. But there is little of the inner strength, the

25

strength of honesty and integrity. American man has lost his center, so he is at sea.

In the Catholic Church there are additional influences from the American Catholic culture. Our Catholic culture is highly clericalized and monasticized. The culture says that priests and religious are holy and about holy things. The laity are just laity, and not much is expected of them. If people really want to be about the business of Church, then they should become priests or religious. Then, too, Roman Catholic culture has been obsessed for centuries with sex. Priests and religious renounce sex, so becoming holy in this culture is connected to doing without sex. Married folks, then, really can't aspire to holiness. They have to be content with second-class membership.

Robert Kinast begins a book on the theology of lay ministry with a quote from Pope Pius X in 1906:

> In the hierarchy alone reside the right and authority of moving and directing the members toward the established goal of the society, whereas it is the duty of the multitude to let itself be governed and to follow obediently the lead of its directors.

Pay, pray, and obey.

The pre-Vatican II Church spoke the language of Thomistic theology. The clergy were trained in abstract philosophy and theology, where reason rules supreme and feelings were suspect and suppressed. It was the theology of the complete system, with answers for everything. Any other way of thinking was not only unnecessary but wrong.

Seminaries were designed to produce celibates, not saints. The rules and customs were formed around fear of women and of homosexuality. Friendships were actively discouraged. Women were forbidden. Group activities were encouraged, but not with the laity, who might taint them. This, of course, produced an elitist group that was inexperienced with and afraid of women and "ordinary people."

The structures, procedures and attitudes of the pre-Vatican II Church were southern-European-feudal, with heavy doses of papalism, centralism, clericalism, monasticism, and patriarchy.

The first Vatican Council (in the 1870's) spelled out some of the functions of the papacy. It was supposed to address the role of bishops, clergy and laity, but

27

never got around to it because its members fled from Garibaldi, who was marching on Rome. As a result, we have what I call "papalism," a one-sided account of the role of the pope without the balance of where the rest of the Church fits in. This dominated the perception of the papacy until Vatican II. It would be similar to defining the role of the president of the United States without spelling out the roles of the Congress and the judiciary and the people.

The highly centralized Roman Catholic Church had been growing for centuries. One decisive step was the Council of Trent, which legislated a uniform liturgy for the first time. Another decisive step occurred with the promulgation of a uniform and universal code of canon law in 1917, also a first.

The Roman Catholic Church was also fundamentalist, not only biblically, but with regard to Church pronouncements. Everything was clear and definite and rigidly authoritarian. We simply took for granted that whatever the Church taught was right. The only attempt to challenge that fundamentalism was denounced as "Modernism" in the early 1900's.

The story of the American version of the pre-Vatican II Church was one of onward and upward. Through the 1940's the American Church was ethnic and neighborhood. Priests and nuns were everywhere and taken for granted. The vast majority of Catholics were in the northeast quadrant of the United States and in the cities. Almost everyone had a chance to go to a parochial school.

Catholics knew who they were by the rules they followed: no meat on Friday, Mass on Sunday, frequent confession, first communion classes, Forty Hours, sodalities, Holy Name societies, May processions, devotions of all kinds.

What kind of Christians were we? How did we relate to God? Devotions—we had a lot of devotions, with the rosary as number one. Our piety, too, was deeply affected by the Catholic form of puritanism called Jansenism. (Because we are American, we have also been affected by puritanism.) The American hierarchy had been strongly influenced by the Irish priests and bishops. Seminary staff and most of the religious communities of women were of French and Irish

29

background, so we were shaped by French and Irish Jansenist piety.

Jansenism (heretical, by the way) concentrated on the divinity of Jesus, the godliness of God, and the sinfulness of the rest of us. Jesus was to be adored in the Blessed Sacrament, not to be approached by us sinners. Sin was everywhere, so there were to be frequent examinations of conscience, acts of contrition, and confession. Communion was not frequent, and some taught (wrongly) that no one should go to communion without going to confession first, just to make sure that we would not receive unworthily.

Since, in our sinfulness, we dared not approach God, who judged our sinfulness, we developed devotions to the saints and Mary, who carried some weight with God. In the forties, during the War, our churches were full for evening devotions (though they were not so in the morning for Mass).

In the forties we were still trying to show that we could be good Americans even though we were Catholics. Catholic men and women in the Armed Forces did a lot for that cause. Then, in the fifties we had Bishop Sheen on TV. The Catholic population was booming. We were building school after school. Young people were entering seminaries and convents in record numbers. Then John Kennedy was elected president. The sun shone brightly on American Catholicism and God smiled down on us from heaven.

If you are not fifty or older, you probably have no idea of what those times were like. They are worth talking about, though, because most of the clergy in this country were formed in those days, and so were many of the rest of today's Church leaders.

In the fifties, too, John XXIII became pope. Almost instantly he became and throughout his tenure remained a beloved Christian leader. He was human. He wanted to tear down the walls of division and build bridges. He was about the business of compassion and forgiveness. He asked us to stop condemning and start looking for common ground on which we could build together.

By the time John became pope, the Church had really become worldwide. Under Pius XII bishops had been appointed all over the Third World. It was clear that there were problems in trying to bring Christ to

31

the Third World in the cultural baggage of a southern-European-feudal Church that still spoke Latin. At least as important was the collapse of European Christianity since the war. While American Catholicism was booming, Europeans had turned their backs on the Church at least in part because of its failure to provide leadership against the Nazis and the Holocaust.

John called the Second Vatican Council to look again at how well we were doing as a Church in being disciples of Jesus.

The Second Vatican Council involved about two thousand eight hundred bishops from almost every country in the world. It was the first really worldwide council ever held. The bishops, to a man (literally, "man"), had become bishops because they were conservatives (half of them were over the age of sixty-five); they could be relied upon to receive what was given to them and pass it on unchanged. They proceeded to change our whole perception of the Roman Catholic Church.

They set into motion radical changes in the way we worship together, the way we think and talk about ourselves as Christians, the way decisions are made. They altered our relationship with other Christians and non-Christians. They affirmed religious liberty and the primacy of individual conscience. They astounded themselves.

The biggest change was the change in language, biggest because the most powerful. When you change the way you talk, you change the way you perceive, the way you see and experience. The bishops (with the help of their theologians) measured the Church against the teachings of Jesus. Abandoning the language of Thomistic theology, they used biblical language.

We together are the people of God, they said, a pilgrim people. Because we share the Spirit of God equally through baptism, we all stand equally before God, and there are no special states or classes of holiness. All are called to holiness. The gifts and ministries of the Spirit are not limited to some but given to all for building up the body of Christ.

Three observations: First, so drastic are the changes which Vatican II began that we are only beginning to come to grips with them. Secondly, Vatican II itself

33

was only a beginning. The new vision could hardly be clearly articulated the first time around. Thirdly, I want to draw attention to the immense fact of a changing Church in the context of many other changes in our world which have affected the way we understand what it is to be Christian and Catholic. Let me come at it in another way.

In America, the sixties brought not only Jack Kennedy but Martin Luther King, Johnson and the War on Poverty. Christians and atheists hit the streets. To be a Christian was to care about the poor and to do something about it. The unmasking of prejudice and the eruption of civil strife, the emergence of the Flower Children and the assassination of Kennedy and King—all of these things affected us deeply. Add to it the war in Vietnam, the growing protest against it, the revolt of youth and the disintegration of their dreams, and the beginnings of the women's movement.

For Catholics, add the mass exodus of priests and nuns, Paul VI's encyclical on birth control, challenges to injustice and prejudice within the Church, resistance to change, and the resulting polarization.

The late sixties saw the proliferation of new catechisms, nuns shedding their habits, experimentation with liturgies. In the seventies the exodus of priests and nuns continued. Catholic schools were being closed down, the feminist movement picked up steam, religious education programs began to replace the schools, parish councils were tried, the Charismatic Movement swept across the country, Catholics were dropping out of the Church, and vocations to the priesthood and to religious communities plummeted.

Biblical studies were changing so rapidly that no one could keep up with them. The same with new theologies.

The sixties and seventies saw the destruction of respect for authority in America, across the board. One thing after another produced a distrust of leadership—the "establishment"—a distrust that included and still includes Church leadership.

Beginning in the fifties, there developed another factor which radically changed American Catholic life: the breakdown of the ethnic church and the neighborhood church, and the emergence of the suburban church.

Church in the new parishes no longer felt the same. The third generation of immigrant families had become Americanized. The ethnic community glue had disappeared.

Response to the changes since Vatican II have varied. Parishes differ widely in their response, and people have been parish-hopping until they find a parish where they are comfortable. Uniformity has disappeared.

The American clergy are disappearing, too. Their average age is in the middle fifties. Predictions are that by the year 2000 the American Church will have less than half the clergy it has now, and they will be much older. We already have "priestless parishes."

Since the Council, American Catholic colleges and universities have begun granting degrees in theology and ministry, some the equivalent of the education of the clergy. Some bishops have begun using these graduates in pastoral roles both in order to satisfy the right of the people to pastoral leadership and to help an aging clergy who have been given more and more to do.

Another interesting factor is the emergence of the American bishops as leaders. Prior to Vatican II we heard little about or from the bishops. They showed up for confirmation and occasionally condemned a movie. Vatican II reaffirmed their pastoral role, their rights as bishops. Following the lead of the Central and South American bishops at Medellin, the United States bishops have spoken out on a variety of issues. They have done this jointly. Individually, their performance has been as even as in any other area of the Church.

Finally, consider, too, the development of international commerce, which has cost American jobs and exploited the poor of the Third World. Consider Reaganomics, which has resulted in a vast increase in the number of the poor and homeless, the increasing feminization of poverty, practically unlimited spending for the military, unbelievable trade deficits and national debt.

This little foray into American and Catholic culture is meant to draw attention to the many ways we are shaped by those cultures. I have obviously only skimmed the surface. What I touched on was too long and too short, but I think it is sufficient to make a point: we are more American and Catholic than we are Christian. What's more, each of us receives his culture in different ways. But who among us is not affected by the great American values of comfort, convenience, mobility, privacy, and greed? Who among us is not affected by American individualism?

What I am trying to get us to notice is how much and how deeply we are affected by our culture. Our culture tells us to work so we can have comforts, the right kind of home in the right place, nice things in the home, nice clothes, vacations, the right car. We feel we have a right to all this and we measure our self-worth in these terms. Some people work two jobs, and their spouses also work to get these things. Immense strains develop within ourselves and in our relationships. The teachings and example of Jesus seem irrelevant to what really matters. What really matters is earning and providing and having.

Then, too, what we have been describing is a world and a Church undergoing increasingly rapid change. We have all been affected by it. Some welcome it. Some begrudgingly yield to the fact or the need.

Some refuse change either by militancy or by indifference. They can't handle it. Their psyches filter out or distort everything that would threaten their world.

Lots of folks have left the Catholic Church to join fundamentalist groups. Some have remained and maintained the Catholic fundamentalism of an earlier time. What is the attraction? It is not biblical and it is not theological. Quite simply, it is psychological. In fundamentalism one finds absolute authority and, therefore, dependency. There is also a kind of clarity: things are black and white and simple. It used to be that way in the Church. It isn't that way anymore, so let's find a *Church* that is that way.

The exodus or retreat to fundamentalism has nothing to do with discipleship. It is an escape from discipleship, an escape from responsibility, a flight to idolatrous dependency. In the time of Jesus some asked, "We have the Law and Abraham. What need do we have of you?"

Lots of folks, too, are upset at criticism of Church leadership. It has to do with the way they learned what it is to be Catholic (culture). It is not a question

39

of truth or discipleship. It is a matter of idolatry of authority and security in dependence.

Jesus harshly criticized the religious leaders of his people. He did it clearly, forcefully, and publicly. Paul criticized Peter publicly and later, for those who had missed it, he brought it up again in one of his letters.

All through Christian history Church leaders have been criticized—usually because they needed to be. Church leaders are not idols. They are people, people like you and me. They are more or less educated and more or less converted to Jesus. In understanding, judgment and experience they are as limited as other human beings. It is idolatrous to think of them in any other way.

Christians, too, know that there is no special state of life that is holy to the exclusion of others. Clericalized and monasticized Catholic culture has taught that "real" holiness is for priests and religious, especially because these states of life are supposed to be free of sex.

Christians know that all life is sacred. American and Catholic culture relegate the sacred to the church building or to shrines. Especially sacred is the Mass.

Recently I asked some Catholics when they pray. All but one answered: when they go to church, before Mass. *Before* Mass! *Praying is something you do in church. You say your own prayers. Father says Mass.*

How many Catholics want to celebrate something and to have Mass as the whole or part of the celebration? Why? Because Catholic culture is clericalized: what the priest does is holy. Nothing else is.

Who is it that gathers in our church buildings each week? What are we like? What sort of people are we arranging liturgies for? What do they bring? What do they need? My point is that we are more American and Catholic than we are disciples of Christ.

I want to conclude my treatment of this point with a more extensive reflection on just one more cultural bias (both American and ecclesial). This can be done for any of the points I've made and lots of others that you can think of. I offer the following as an example. The topic is the way we relate to women.

In America, of the four hundred and twenty job classifications listed by the United States Government, 80% of employed American women are in the lowest twenty job classes—no benefits, no retirement. Of those who sell apparel, for example, 83% are women, earning an average of $171 a week. On the other hand, of those selling cars and boats, 91% are men, earning an average of $400 a week.

Two-thirds of the elderly women in America live below the poverty line—two thirds!

Under current Social Security legislation, if a wife dies, the husband continues to collect full benefits. If the husband dies, the widow' benefits are cut almost in half. This is the feminization of poverty in America.

Two million women a year are subject to physical beatings in America. Wives are beaten in two-thirds of marriages; one-fourth of American wives are beaten weekly. One woman in America is physically beaten every eighteen seconds. One is raped every seven minutes.

We are talking about our mothers and grandmothers, wives, daughters and granddaughters. Is it worth talking about? Are there issues here of justice and love?

Patriarchal society has been with us a long time. Prophets among us are confronting us with its evils. It is sinful. It took Christians nineteen centuries to face the evils of slavery. Now it is time to look at the sinful way we treat women. Look at the ways we resist. We are not interested in the teachings and actions of Jesus. We clutch at straws and distort scripture to justify our resistance. I don't intend here to review all the scriptural and theological arguments for the equality of women. All of that has been done *ad nauseam,* and all who want to examine their cultural biases can easily find those studies. There are simply no arguments left to justify the failure to treat women equally. Not to do so is sinful.

The Roman Catholic record is both inspiring and scandalous. Men and women of the Church have listened to the Spirit, who spoke first from outside the

43

Church. They listened and repented. Others, including some in leadership, are resisting the Spirit, and that is scandalous. Strong words, but they need to be said, and they will continue to be said until we all repent.

Do we have people leading and participating in our liturgies who are more influenced by this cultural bias than by Jesus? You bet we do.

The question here—and it is important to know what the question is—Is this call for the equal treatment of women really a prophetic call, the work of the Spirit, or not?

The biggest question facing the early Church was whether or not to admit gentiles into the Church without also requiring them to accept Judaism and the Law. Paul was already doing it. Peter had already had the experience of the Spirit coming to Cornelius and his household. The leadership of the Church gathered in Jerusalem to discuss the issue. It is very instructive to look at *how* they decided it. They did *not* look at their long Jewish tradition. They did *not* look at the probable consequences of their decision. They looked at the *source* of the issue. They said,

"The *Spirit* and we have decided . . . " This is of the Spirit, they said, so we'll do what God wants.

"It is not so simple today," we hear—smokescreen. "It could create some serious problems," we hear— evasion. "It's not the right time," we hear—resist- ance. Are we disciples of patriarchy or disciples of Jesus? Jesus was crucified. Are we afraid of hard times and pain? Jesus bore witness to the truth. Can disciples of Jesus do less?

Where is courage today? Where is wisdom? Where is discipleship?

Power is at stake here, of course. But what has hap- pened to the powerlessness of a crucified savior and a Paul who would glory in his weakness?

When Jesus is before Pilate in John's Gospel, Pilate asks Jesus if he is a king. Jesus responds: "For this did I come into the world, to bear witness to the truth." The truth is the source of the authority of Je- sus. It must be so for his disciples. The truth of Je- sus is a way of life, a living word, a word fleshed out—not words in a book or a creed.

We, the disciples of Jesus, are filled with the Spirit so that *we* can be that word made flesh in our flesh. We are to be the light of truth. If the salt loses it power, with what will it be flavored?

The Holocaust and Naziism, slavery and religious wars have been partly the responsibility of "Christians" who were not willing to sacrifice themselves to save others. The statistics I cited earlier are at least partly our responsibility. It is *our* grandmothers, mothers, wives, children and grandchildren who will continue to be sacrificed on the altar of patriarchy if we continue to do nothing.

We who gather for liturgy are more American and Catholic than we are disciples of Jesus. We have to face this if our liturgies are ever to become what they are supposed to be.

In the late sixties a then-Jesuit theologian, Charles Davis, wrote to the effect that in the past the Church was renewed by saints; today we try to get by with spiritual operators. The difference is real. Spiritual operators are do-gooders, trying this gimmick and that. Saints are people who are converted to Christ, and whose entire perception of life is governed by their ongoing relationship with Christ.

Kierkegaard knew well the difference between the aesthetic and the religious. It is so easy to mix them up, especially in liturgy. We can easily be satisfied with good performances, good art, good music, good symbols. If we are satisfied with that, then we have missed the point. The point is *do we experience God?*

Are we who gather each week for worship really Christian or are we members of the Church? What I am talking about here, of course, is conversion to Christ. As I said earlier, one of the ways we have been formed by our Catholic culture is the sense that real holiness is for priests and religious (never mind that priests say it's for sisters and monks, and they say it's for great saints, and so we pass the buck). To find out how deeply ingrained is the aversion to holiness, tell a group of people that they are called to be holy and ask them how they feel about it. The response, expressed in many ways, boils down to "You're adding something on to what I've learned. I can get to heaven without all that, can't I?" There is

47

immense confusion about what it is to be holy and what it is to be a disciple of Jesus.

Another way of describing discipleship is conversion, *continuous conversion.* How is a Christian different from a non-Christian? How is one's life affected by being baptized into Christ? Different answers come from different sources, but being converted to Christ means at least that we are constantly being called to die to whatever is not of God so that we can rise to newer life in God. Conversion is never finished. We come to God again and again as we are, flawed and limited, with a history of unexamined assumptions and cherished beliefs and values. We come again and again with buried fears and guilt and pain. Little by little, ever so slowly, we submit to the light of Christ, who has come to set us free, to heal us, to launch us into bringing about God's reign.

Conversion is impossibly complex. At least four dimensions are in constant interaction: affective, moral, intellectual, and religious. If I am converted to Jesus (religious), then it affects everything about me: my feelings and felt values (affective), my choices and actions (moral), and my thinking, what I think about, and how I think and reflect (intellectual).

To be a disciple of Jesus is to love God and my neighbor with all my heart (affective) and all my mind (intellectual) by living his word (moral).

It is all too easy to feel strongly about something without ever examining whether it has anything at all to do with being a disciple of Jesus. It is all too easy to be convinced of something while refusing honest questions and any thoughts or viewpoints that might make us reevaluate it. Yet, this is the very stuff of conversion, of discipleship. It is in the confrontation with the Gospel of Jesus and with our pains and failures that we discover our resistance and rebelliousness, our ignorance and fear. It is to this journey that Jesus calls us. He summons us to the adventure of wrestling with God. He comes again and again to set us free, to love us into wholeness.

Reflection with Jesus is a part of that adventure, but not the whole of it. We are not into navel-gazing. Reflection with Jesus leads us to the choices and actions that bring about God's reign. We become the word made flesh, a light to the world.

49

The degree of conversion (salvation) depends on the whole "language" of the community of faith that calls us to conversion. By "language" I mean not only the words used, but the way Christian life is lived by that particular community of faith. It is primarily that lived experience which teaches us what it is to be Christian.

People involved in religious education have got to be concerned with liturgy and the whole life of the parish. This is the primary teacher. This is the local cultural influence that defines the meaning of the words used in instruction. I wish I had a nickel for everyone who said, "I went all through Catholic grammar school and high school and never experienced Jesus until I made a Cursillo" or retreat or whatever. If religious educators narrowly confine themselves to instruction, they are doing only half the job. Meaning comes from the combination of symbol (word) and *experience*. It we teach only the words and don't provide the experiences, we get the complaint: "I don't get anything out of it. It doesn't mean anything to me." If parish religious educators teach liturgy in the classroom, they had better see to it that their weekend liturgies are like that as well.

It is primarily that lived experience which teaches us what it is to be Christian. I heard a story some years ago. A man had been asked to be a godparent at his nephew's baptism. He was required to get a letter from his pastor testifying that he was a Catholic in good standing. He went to the pastor, who checked the financial records. Sure enough, the man had come to church each week and turned in his envelope. The pastor was happy to say that this man was indeed a Catholic in good standing!

Isn't it true that, not only in the past but even today, Christianity is experienced as compatible with greed, ambition, hatred, violence, patriarchy, materialism, impersonalism, selfishness, indifference, apathy, and prejudice—among other things? That's the way some "Christians" are, and few seem to mind.

Some years ago I attended a conference for priests. The speaker was a priest who did and continues to do important work for the American bishops. He has also been editor of an influential religious magazine. He began his remarks by offhandedly saying that he wasn't particularly pious. Did he feel that by admitting his lack of piety the priests present would

51

identify better with him? Is lukewarmness what God really wants for us and for his world?

When I talk about piety, I do not mean the neurotic, bigoted, one-dimensional fanaticism which is an escape from responsibility. Jesus was fairly clear, I think: "Seek first the reign of God and his justice. Love the Lord your God with all your heart and soul and strength and mind."

There are those among us, though, who don't want to press this too far. Part of the resistance, I am sure, comes from the cultural bias that holiness is for someone else and I can get by without it.

Not too long ago I attended another meeting for clergy. Once again the speaker was a well-known author and priest. One of the things he talked about was dealing with "marginal Catholics," the ones who seldom, if ever, "go to church." He asked, "What do you do when they show up at the rectory asking to be married or have their baby baptized?" His solution was to read some saying of Jesus' about love and compassion, and then *deliberately* and *explicitly* to say that he didn't want to read any of the hard sayings because that would confound the argument. Then he told some stories of people who eventually came back to church and were grateful that they hadn't been turned away before.

He then invoked the priests present to discuss what they did with these "marginal Catholics." The common response was to be "nice."

We really don't believe that we are called to holiness. Let's not offend anyone. Especially, let's not remember Jesus talking about the narrow way or the cross or denying ourselves. Let's not remember that people took offense at Jesus and walked away from him. Let's not remember that Jesus would not compromise.

We really don't believe that we are called to holiness. We don't believe that we are called to repent of our lukewarmness or that we should call anyone else to repent. We feel very uncomfortable asking of others what we do not ask of ourselves.

Do not make demands on "marginal Catholics." Be nice. Be loving and kind. But not calling for repentance is not at all loving. We mistake softness for love, but love is firm and strong and committed.

Love exists, grows, and flourishes in the truth. Love is not wishy-washy and soft. Love at its heart is made of steel.

The way of Jesus was prepared for by John the Baptist, whose message was "Repent." Mark tells us that Jesus began his own work by taking up where John left off. "Repent," he said, "the kingdom of God is at hand." He continued to call us to be sincere and truthful, to die to ourselves, to pick up our crosses. When Peter said he didn't like that very much, Jesus said: "Get behind me, you satan."

Jesus called us to respond to God's passionate love for us with all our heart and soul and strength and mind. Nothing less works, nothing less saves, nothing less sets us free. Jesus continued to call us to accept him and what he said and did as food and drink, as life-giving. At the end he had very few disciples.

The first reading on Palm Sunday comes to mind here. It is from Isaiah, Chapter 50:

> The Lord has given me a well-trained tongue, that I might know how to speak to the weary a word that will rouse them. Morning after morning he opens my ear that I might hear; and I have not rebelled, have not turned back. I gave my back to those who beat me,

> my cheeks to those who plucked my beard, my face I
> did not shield from buffets and spitting. The Lord God
> is my help, therefore I am not disgraced; I have set my
> face like flint, knowing that I shall not be put to
> shame.

The heart of love, like Jesus' love, is made of steel.

In recent years Catholic periodicals have had articles that again and again claim that we ask too much of those seeking Baptism and Confirmation. We are solemnly reminded that the Catholic Church, after all, has always been the Church of "everyone," a "wheat field filled with weeds." Those criticizing the catechumenate ask, "Are we creating a class of super-Catholics?" Those criticizing high school Confirmation say that we should not demand commitment of our youth at the very time that they are sorting out their values.

Of course, we are a wheat field filled with weeds—individually and collectively. We are a Church of elders and beginners, of saints and sinners, of the rebellious and the passive. We are not a Church of the perfect, but a pilgrim people, a people on a journey together. But that does not mean that the demand for continual repentance and growth are not there or that the values are not clear.

As for those who misread adolescent psychology to provide an excuse for delaying commitment, they miss the point that it is only *within* the framework of commitment that values can be sorted out at all. That is precisely what is healing and integrating and life-giving in the teaching of Jesus: "Seek first the reign of God."

I am reminded of so many instances, which, I am sure, are part of your own experience. I have had teachers who demanded little of their students and got what they asked for. I have had teachers who demanded a lot, who called for the best we had. We not only learned more from them, but we also remember them with fondness.

The American Catholic Church is soft. We settle for being nice instead of being loving. We confuse discipleship with membership. We settle for mediocrity and we get it. We have empty liturgical performances instead of life-giving gatherings of worshipping communities.

The first task of those concerned with liturgy is the continuing call to repentance, conversion. I want to explore this some more.

The degree of conversion to Christ depends on how it is preached and lived. Who is Jesus? What does Jesus ask of us? What does it mean to be initiated into the community of the disciples of Jesus?

For a long time, Catholics used the word *faith* to mean "I agree to that." Christian faith is much more than that. It is not a statement of fact or belief, but a declaration of love, an invitation to a relationship with God.

Jesus reveals God to us. What we see and hear from Jesus is what God is like. Jesus tells us and shows us a God who is passionately in love with his creation and with each of us. Paul gets ecstatic about it when he says "Nothing can separate us from this love that God has for us." The crucifixion is the final and ultimate symbol of that love. All is given when Jesus gives up his life. There is nothing more to give. The message from Jesus on the cross is "You have done your worst to me and you cannot stop me from loving you."

To believe in Jesus is to be confronted by a lover who says: "I love you. What are you going to do about it?"

Jesus invites us into a relationship with him, with God, through the power of the Spirit. It is through that relationship that we become the saints that Charles Davis talked about. It is that relationship that is the difference between the Christian and the non-Christian. It is that relationship that is the foundation of all the rest.

Many in Western civilization have absorbed Christian teachings and Christian values because Western culture has been influenced by Christ. That does not make them Christian. It makes them influenced by Christians.

Jesus says: "Seek first the reign of God and his justice." The justice of God is that he makes us just, by sharing the Spirit, by forgiving our sins, by loving us to wholeness.

Seek the reign of God first, not second, not third. God wants to be at the very center of our lives, what we hunger and thirst for. It is not enough to "go to church" or to be involved in doing good or to be saying "Lord, Lord." Jesus is about the heart. Where is our heart?

The conclusion of the parable of the unjust steward expresses the frustration of Jesus: those who don't know him, those concerned only about themselves and their world are much more industrious and enterprising in seeking their goals than the "children of light" are in seeking his will. What would happen if we put real desire and energy into seeking God?

Some years ago I went out to dinner with three couples. We had spent the day at a religious conference. One of the men began to tell of the small group that he had shared with in the afternoon. Instead of discussing the assigned topic, they had begun to share stories of how they had come to know Jesus. While he was recounting this, he began to cry. He said, "Fifty years of my life have been wasted. These young men in my group already know Jesus and are living for him. I've wasted fifty years of my life."

His wife and friends tried to console him and calm him down (we were in a very public place—a nice restaurant). They said things like "What are you talking about? You've been a good husband and a good father. You go to church and you're a good man." Nothing helped. I said, "You really feel rotten, huh?" He nodded. I said, "Well, that's great. You've had a good day. At least now you can begin. Lots of people don't get that chance. You've had quite a blessing today. Let's celebrate." He bought that.

There are a few lessons here. I said earlier that the depth of conversion is determined, at least in part, by the "language" in which the gospel is transmitted. The "language" includes not only the words but the way in which they are lived by those around us. This man was converted by the people in his group sharing their relationship with God. *They* were the living word of the Gospel.

I remember a time when I was watching some professional tennis players. As I watched, I realized how poorly I played. It was like that with this man. As he listened to how those young men were living with

Christ, he saw how poorly he responded to Christ's love. As he listened to their concern to do God's will, he knew how half-heartedly he sought God's will.

This brings up a second lesson: conversion always means seeing God and one's self and one's life in a new way. What I couldn't see before I see now. I cannot draw close to Jesus, the light of the world, without seeing my sinfulness, my lack of gratitude, my laziness, selfishness, and so on. The difference between the "before" and the "after" is so striking that the "before" is almost always exaggerated as terribly bad. The contrast is found throughout the scriptures. It is the difference between life in the Spirit and life in the flesh, between old wine and new, between darkness and light. It is being born again. Paul exults: "We are new creatures in Christ. We have died with him and risen with him."

Another lesson from this story is that conversions happen over and over again. This man was a good man. He encountered some people who unintentionally brought him to a new openness of heart. He wasn't defensive. He was ready. He responded. We are never finished—Jesus continues to set us free if we let him.

What happened to this man happens to many and, I believe, is by far the most common way of conversion: in response to the living word of others. It is not the only way. We are touched by God unexpectedly—as Paul was, on the way to Damascus. Some are moved when alone at prayer, reading or in touch with nature.

The point is that this is the foundation of the Christian life: encounter with God. I have experienced his presence and his love for me. God is not simply God-out-there, but *my God*.

Conversions come in big and little steps. Big ones are powerful experiences. We remember all the details of when and where. Our lives change, and we find new energy. On the other hand, conversions come in little ways, so small we hardly notice. I know a lot of mature Christians who cannot remember any big moments. They have grown into who they are little by little.

Conversion to Jesus, then, is a lifelong struggle. Over and over again we have to decide to respond to God's love. What form does that decision take? What does it look like? What does it mean?

Someone told me once that she felt like a piece of Swiss cheese, with the holes being her incompleteness. Some of those voids were filled with achievements. Some, with friends and people she loved. But the greatest void could be filled only with God.

The decision to respond to God's love takes the form of choosing Jesus to be the most important person in my life. It is you, Jesus, whom I will seek with all my heart and soul and strength and mind. I put my life in your hands. I trust that in seeking you I will find you. I trust that you will lead me into the heart of God. I no longer want to be self-sufficient. I want to seek first your reign, your will for me. I want to stop trying to run my life and seek your way of living.

The decision to respond to God's love is a rejection both of self-sufficiency (an illusion, anyhow) and of the gods I invent which I can control or fit into *my* life as *I* want to live it. The decision is an act of faith, as are all decisions to love. I don't know where it will lead. I simply trust that casting my lot with Jesus, living in intimacy with him, being his disciple and living life his way will bring me abundant life. I trust that, instead of just partly living, I will become truly alive.

Recently, I received a letter which puts it this way:

> I didn't know what this business of God loving me was all about—or why Christ died for us, but I'm beginning to, and I finally *do* know why I always felt so alone, so isolated and scared—I had no connectedness to God—and now I'm no longer hanging on by a golden thread, but feel a flooding—in and out of light, strength and love. I acknowledge my connection. I didn't actually know until recently that one could develop a personal relationship with God through prayer and that simply by asking him to be part of your life, he would.

What does the decision to respond to God's love mean? Well, it means that I will find the time to be alone with Jesus to share. With him, as his disciple, I will reflect on every aspect of my life in the light of his teachings. I will search the scriptures with him so that I may get to know him better and so that I may get to know his teachings better. This is the hardest part because it demands honesty and change. Neither do I find easy.

Obviously, the decision to respond to God's love for me involves immediately a setting of priorities. If I'm not fooling myself, the choice to respond to God's love with all my heart and soul and strength and mind absolutely requires that I set aside time to be alone with him to share. I absolutely must also find time to reflect with him on his word in the scriptures. If I don't do this, then my word is empty and nothing will happen.

One of the concerns of some American Catholic laity today has been expressed as a desire to receive teaching on how to bring their faith into their lives outside of the church building and church activities. The concern is admirable, but it can also be a symptom of the cultural compartmentalizing of the sacred and the secular. Response to the concern is not to be found in endless attempts at "Christian" solutions to endless varieties of life situations. What is needed is a deeper understanding of what it means to be converted to Christ. As we become people of prayer and as we reflect on our lives in the light of his teachings, we will know what to do.

I know people who take dieting seriously. I know others who work at physical fitness. They have established priorities and they stick to what they have decided on. They think about what they are doing. They work at it. They put their time and energy into it, and it pays off.

On the other hand, I know lots and lots of people who say they want to do something about their weight or about getting into shape but who never get around to it. Do they really want to change?

I would like to pause here to get our bearings. This is a book about liturgy. This discussion of discipleship and conversion is in the context of the question: Who are we who gather for worship? This is the most basic question and concern of liturgy. If what we do when we gather is the work of the worshipping community and not just the business of the priest, then we have to be concerned with the preparation of the people (and of the presider). What we do most of the time is try to pretend we have an orchestra—with people who can't play their instruments.

We take for granted that those who come for our weekly gathering are prepared. Or we simply ignore the question. I have found it almost impossible to engage liturgists in a discussion about it. Let's talk instead about what music to use or how to create a good procession or how to train lectors. In fact, however, unless we address the issue, we are producing empty performances which achieve nothing.

I contend that our parish churches are filled with people who are more American and Catholic than Christian. It is, and has been from the beginning, a problem of the second generation and of growth. Faith and discipleship cannot be passed on. The context can be created in which faith can be chosen. Religious instruction and behavior can be taught, but they provide only the context. The decision of faith must be made by each one. This is the second generation problem. The fact that a child is raised in a believing family and exposed to the Church and to religious instructions does not mean that the child will be a believer. Somewhere along the line we must decide for ourselves.

The decision to follow Christ, as we have discussed above, is not a once-and-for-all decision. So, the problem of growth. As there are stages of childhood and adolescence, so there are stages of adult growth. And there are stages of faith growth.

People who gather each week for our liturgies come from all these places. They are waiting to be called forth. They are hungry. We give them performances.

The Church in America is known for its movements: the Cursillo, the Charismatic Renewal, Marriage Encounter, and so forth. It is pretty well documented that the vast majority of people active in their parishes come from the movements. People who have been involved in these movements say, "Why didn't we get this in our parishes?" At the end of a weekend retreat the Mass is always a wonderful celebration, and inevitably the question is asked, "Why can't Mass be like this in our parish?" Ever since I became involved with Teens Encounter Christ and the Cursillo in Chicago in the sixties, I have asked myself the same questions.

We come back to some questions we started with. What we do in our liturgies depends on what we understand by the term *Church*. What are we for as Church? What sorts of things are we concerned with as Church? How are we Church? What sorts of things do we do as Church?

If people say: "I don't get anything out of going to Mass," we need to listen. If the movements have flourished, we need to ask ourselves why people had to go out of their parishes to find God.

There have, of course, been parish renewal programs like RENEW that have produced wonderful results in the parishes. And there are Bible sharing groups and parish missions, and so on. These are all good things. We all need a shot in the arm every now and then. But why doesn't what these things are about happen through our weekly meetings together? We get together *every week*. Do we really need more than one meeting a week?

I know that there are many different models of Church. I've settled on my own: to be Church is to be a community of disciples of Jesus whose business is to bring about the reign of God. That makes the primary purpose of the parish to grow disciples of Jesus. Let's use everything we can, of course, but let's not stop asking ourselves why more doesn't happen through our weekly meetings.

The last section of this book is concerned with what we do at our weekly meetings. Let me close this reflection by insisting again that if we want our liturgies to work, we have to work at the continual call to repentance (conversion).

The bishops have also said that for the liturgical reform to work, not only must it be the work of the disciples of Jesus, but we must be people of prayer. A parish, then, is also a place where people learn to pray. In the past, we have taught people prayers. Now we need to teach them to pray. In the past, Father said Mass, Father was the celebrant. Now we come together to stand together before God.

Meeting Jesus, letting in his presence and love, is a beginning. Where the relationship goes depends on all the things that affect human relationships. Jesus is always with us. That is his promise to us: "I'll be with you." It is the promise of God in the Jewish scriptures: "I'll be with you." The most common complaint of God is "You don't listen, you don't notice; you have eyes and you don't see, you have ears and you don't hear."

The heart of any relationship is communication. The twin foundations of communication are truth (honesty) and presence. Let's begin with presence. Have you ever tried to talk to someone, and you feel like you're talking to a brick wall? You know the other person is not paying attention. That's an easy way to say "presence": paying attention in the present. Paying attention here and now means concentration: I really want to hear what you are saying and I want to notice how you are saying it. I'm not just hearing, I'm listening. I'm not carrying a lot of baggage into this moment. I'm present to you right now. I want to understand you and what you are telling me.

The baggage we can carry into an encounter can be a desire to argue or convince or change the other. It might be fear, images I don't want to let go of, ideas I don't want challenged.

Before a bond can develop between myself and another, we have to be able to be present to each other, able to give undivided attention to each other. Intimacy is the name we give to the experience of that kind of communication. What was hidden inside of me is now between us because I have shared myself with you. I have trusted you with myself. What was hidden inside of you is no longer just inside of you, but between us because you have shared it with me. You have trusted me with yourself. Intimacy is possible only to the extent that such sharing goes on.

What is true of my relationship with any other human being is also true of my relationship with Jesus and God (Father, Mother, etc.). The relationship begins with the encounter and grows through the times we take to be alone together to share. All three things are necessary: taking time, being alone together, sharing.

I recently read somewhere the story of a New England couple. Over the years, the wife would ask her husband, "Do you love me?" The husband never responded. One day she asked the same question, "Do you love me?" To her amazement he stopped and looked at her. "At last," she thought, "he's going to tell me he loves me." Instead, he said, "I told you that twenty years ago. If I change my mind, I'll tell you."

Every twenty years is really not enough. Things become real to us because we symbolize them and put them into words. Symbols (like words) complete the meaning, make it "more real." Have you ever noticed how much more real your own sin is when you put it into words: "I lied, I stole, I cheated."

It is not enough for us to hear someone else say that God loves us. We need to hear God himself say it to our hearts. We need to *say* it to God. Only then does it become "real" for us.

To grow in our relationship with God, we need to take time out to be alone together to share. If we don't, the relationship never develops. God will remain a stranger, out there somewhere, not really *my* God, *my* Savior.

Jesus prayed because he had to. He had to put into words who he was and what he felt. He also had to listen to the Father. They had to be present to each other for their intimacy to grow. That is what prayer is and what prayer is for and why the spreading of the gospel was always accompanied by the exhortation to pray. Paul says, "Pray always."

Prayer beings with presence. I take time out to be alone with God. I relax and clear my mind. I acknowledge the presence of Jesus and the Father. I say, "Jesus (or Father, Mother, etc.), here I am." I ask the Spirit to make me aware of God's presence. Sometimes I might say, over and over, the name I have for God. That is the beginning of prayer: becoming aware of the presence of God. I don't always feel it, but I do most of the time. When I don't feel it, I affirm it.

To me, prayer is always dialogue—at least as much listening as speaking. I pay attention to my heart. When I speak, I may go through a litany of thanksgiving. I may ask for something. I may share my fears or anger or frustration or joy. I may ask for insight or forgiveness.

It is in these times of being alone together with God that we are changed, strengthened, challenged, humbled, forgiven. It is this constantly renewed self that we bring to the world and to the people around us as we pay attention to them.

This is not a treatise on prayer, nor is it intended to be. By now, however, you will have noticed that I have drawn attention to those dimensions of prayer that are necessary if we are to pray the liturgy: presence, honesty, thanksgiving and listening.

Earlier I mentioned a survey I did, asking people when they prayed. I've done this many times, and only one person out of hundreds indicated that liturgy was prayer. Most of us identify praying with saying prayers. Hardly anyone thinks of liturgy as prayer. We sing, we listen to readings, we make responses, we go to communion—and Father says Mass.

Father Eugene Walsh says somewhere that the primary principle of liturgy is that everyone who comes should have at least the opportunity of experiencing God. Everything we do must be subordinated to that principle. Anything that takes away from it is out of place. This is another way of saying that our liturgies are the times when we come together to stand before God. We allow ourselves to be present to each other, to speak and to listen.

All of this will become much clearer in Part Three, but, for now, it seems to me that we have a lot of work to do. Those responsible for preparing and presiding over liturgies must themselves be people of prayer. If we don't know how to pray, how can we prepare liturgies that are prayerful? If we don't know how to make our liturgies prayerful, we make them artistic.

It is not enough, though, that those who prepare liturgies be prayerful. We have to teach our people to pray. They are the celebrants, the worshipping community. If we are to get beyond the experience of a people attending the priest's Mass and become a worshipping community, then we must teach the community to pray.

I have time and again gone over this with the people of my parish. I have explained what it means for us to come before God together, how we must be silent and let our hearts notice God's presence with us. I tell them how to listen to their hearts in the silences so that they can "hear" God speak to them. We do take time to be silent together—but more about this in Part Three.

Before moving on to look at where we are going and what we might do at our weekly meeting, there are two more things that require some attention: the Holy Spirit and the community we call the Church. Since the Church is the community of those united in Spirit, I'll discuss them together.

The pre-Vatican II Church paid little attention to the Holy Spirit. In 1897 Pope Leo XIII noted that we Catholics seem to have overlooked the Holy Spirit. He said in his encyclical *Divinum Illud* that if we were asked whether or not we have received the Holy Spirit, some would answer, "We have not so much as heard whether there be a Holy Spirit." He went on to say that, while we use the name in our prayers, we are very deficient in our knowledge of the Holy Spirit; so he directed preachers and those who had care of souls that it was their duty to instruct their people more diligently and more fully about the Holy Spirit. (We didn't pay a whole lot of attention to that encyclical either.)

Pope Leo asked the whole Church to pray the novena from Ascension Thursday to Pentecost for a new Pentecost in our time, a new outpouring of the Holy

77

Spirit, a new empowering, a new giving of life by the Spirit.

This, too, was the prayer of John XXIII prayed at all Masses before and during the Council. We prayed: "Renew in our days your miracles as of a second Pentecost."

Many of the bishops spoke of the power of the Spirit moving among them during the Council. Pope Paul VI opened the third session in 1964 by saying: "The Spirit is here . . . to illuminate and guide our labors to the benefit of the Church and all mankind. The Spirit is here; we call upon him, wait for him, follow him; the Spirit is here."

That was a solemn and awesome moment: *The Spirit is here.*

In 1966 Paul VI commented on the work of the Spirit in the Church. He said that the action of the Spirit could be diminished or even absent, so

> This is why the Word of God is preached and the sacraments of grace are distributed; this is why people pray and why each individual tries to merit the "great gift of God," the Holy Spirit, for himself and for the whole Church. For this reason, if we really love the

Church, the main thing we must do is to foster in it an outpouring of the divine Paraclete, the Holy Spirit.

This is the heart of it: *if we really love the Church, the main thing we must do is to foster in it an outpouring of the divine Paraclete, the Holy Spirit.* I see this as the job of religious leaders—to bring those who would listen to an openness to the Spirit. The Spirit leads us to Christ, who takes us to the heart of God whom he calls Father. There we are enlightened and cleansed and healed and empowered and sent forth. As we grow and mature, we discover together what the Spirit is gifting each one—and all of us—to do. Here we have reached the "beyond" to which religious structures and practices point.

In all four Gospels Jesus begins a new life after his baptism by John. Before the baptism he was an obscure carpenter from Nazareth. Afterwards he becomes an itinerant preacher so filled with the power of God that his brief ministry changes the whole world.

At the baptism by John the Holy Spirit comes upon Jesus. He is led by the Spirit into the desert. He returns full of the Spirit and power. In Jesus the power of the Spirit is revealed as the power to heal and forgive, the power to speak God's word (prophecy), to give abundant life, to drive out demons, to work miracles. Jesus had become the Christ, the anointed, messiah.

The Spirit of God, the Spirit in/of Jesus is the Spirit of truth, the Spirit who reveals God, the Spirit of love. It is this Spirit who is passed on to us, who empowers us to do as Jesus did.

The passing on of the Spirit occurred in John's Gospel on the day of the resurrection. In Luke, it happened at Pentecost. Jesus came to baptize in the Spirit and in fire. This is the gift promised by the Father. At the beginning of Acts, Jesus tells the disciples to wait in Jerusalem for this gift. They wait and the Spirit comes. The Church is born. The Spirit present in Christ fills the disciples and they become "Christ," the anointed presence of the Spirit in *their* flesh. Paul would say: "We are the body of Christ," the messianic presence. What the Spirit accomplished in Jesus is now to work through us.

The Letter to the Ephesians puts it this way:

> Each one of us has received a special gift in proportion to what Christ has given. It was he who gave gifts to

mankind; he appointed some to be apostles, others to be prophets, others to be evangelists, others to be pastors and teachers. He did this to prepare all God's people for the work of Christian service, in order to build up the body of Christ. And so we shall all come together to that oneness in our faith and in our knowledge of the Son of God; we shall become mature people, reaching to the very height of Christ's full stature . . . by speaking the truth in a spirit of love we must grow up in every way to Christ, who is the head. Under his control all the different parts of the body fit together, and the whole body is held together by every joint with which it is provided. So when each separate part works as it should, the whole body grows and builds itself up in love. (Eph. 4:7, 11-16).

We need to open our hearts to the action of the Spirit, to welcome the power of God. This is what makes us different. The Church is not just a club or an organization, but a people filled with the Spirit of God who wants to reveal his saving power through us. The signs and wonders of the messianic age are meant to be the ordinary life of the disciples. It is the Spirit who gives us faith and hope and love. Through the Spirit we come to know God and the things of God. It is the Spirit who empowers us to pray and to understand scripture.

Paul lists some of the gifts and ministries of the Spirit at work in the community formed by the Spirit: the gift of tongues, interpretation, prophecy, miracles, discernment of spirits, wisdom, and knowledge. There are the ministries of apostle, prophet, healing, administration—whatever is needed to bring about the kingdom.

It is the Spirit we receive at baptism who makes us holy, because holiness means sharing God's own life. Holiness is not goodness. Goodness means following the law. To be holy is to be a temple of the Holy Spirit. Holiness, God's Spirit in us, can coexist with our sin. This is the Good News: God shares his own life with us as pure gift, no strings, no conditions, even though we are and always will be sinners.

Most of us Catholics have not believed what the early Christians believed about the power of the Spirit at work in us. And, because we have not believed, we have not experienced it. We were formed in a Catholic culture which did not include the Spirit. In our catechisms we listed the gifts of the Spirit from the *Old* Testament. Tongues and prophecy, miracles and holiness were not about Catholics. We have made great celebrations of Easter and Christmas, but not Pentecost.

When I was a child in the early forties, I read Captain Marvel comic books. Captain Marvel, you may recall, was a story about a lame boy, Billy Batson, who would become Captain Marvel when he spoke the magic word *SHAZAM*. Each of the letters in *SHAZAM* stood for the "elder gods," like *S* for Solomon and *H* for Hercules. The particular episode I recall was set in the future—in the eighties. People had shortened a lot of words. They said "bod" instead of "body," for example. So Billy Batson shortened *SHAZAM* to *SHAZ*. He was transformed, but this Captain Marvel was slow and timid. By the end of the episode he realized that he had to use the whole word. By leaving out the *AM*, he failed to call on Achilles for courage and Mercury for speed.

Something like that has happened to us in the Church. We have been transformed by baptism, but we lack the power of the Spirit. The Holy Spirit is working in us, of course, or we would not believe. But we have not believed enough. We need to be open to all that God wants for us, to all that God wants us to be for the world. We are God's children through the spirit, his body, the messianic presence.

In his book *Charism and Sacrament,* Father Donald Gelpi, S.J., described the Spirit-gifted Church better than anyone I know. He speaks of the Church as knowing they are a people, why they are a people, and what they are for as a people. To have this shared vision, they need the gift of tongues in their midst to remind them of Pentecost. Tongues is the tie-in with the original experience, the originating experience. Prophecy and interpreted tongues give the Church the experience of the Spirit as a guiding presence. Teaching both keeps the Church aware of its origins and destiny and clarifies what we believe. Healing and miracles authenticate teaching and reveal the abiding love of the Father. Discernment helps the community know which of the impulses of its members needs to be approached in faith. The action gifts, coordinated in love through the gift and skill of leadership, are the expression of the Church's origins, self-awareness and calling to be the messianic presence.

If any of the gifts are missing, not only will our awareness of who we are be diminished, but our life together will be both distorted and crippled. A parish without tongues lacks a sense of its Pentecostal origins. This, in turn, means (among other things) failure to appreciate the work of the Holy Spirit, failure to look for and yield to the Spirit's promptings, and therefore a breeding ground for rationalism, moralism, legalism, and formalism; a loss of the sense of prayer as gift and therefore its replacement by do-it-yourself piety.

Where the gift of prophecy is absent, we lose our sense of being led together by the Lord.

Where the *gift* of teaching is absent, teaching becomes academic, without the call to repentance. At the same time, there will be an exaggerated sense of the importance of emotional experience and a tendency to rely on witness and prophecy to the exclusion of teaching.

Where healing and miracles are absent, there is missing the sense that God is in our midst. God is removed from us rather than being our Emmanuel, God-with-us. Church, then, is no longer the place where God is encountered, but a place for empty ritual duties.

Where authentic discernment is missing, there will be no sense of what God wants, no seeking of his will. Instead there will be directionless activity with little or no efficacy in bringing people to God.

Where the action gifts are missing, there is a closed-in self-centeredness with all its deadening consequences. The life of faith will be more or less abstract and vague.

To be Church, then, is to be a community of the disciples of Jesus, filled with the power of the Spirit to bring about the reign of God. This is what the local Church, the parish, is about. Just by describing it, we can see what its essential concerns must be: continual conversion to Christ, continual conversion to the Holy Spirit, continual conversion to community, continual conversion to the actions that are the kingdom of God.

At the beginning of this book I said that I have rarely run into anyone who appreciates how radical the Council's liturgical reform has been. The Council was not about the business of updating or modernizing or some kind of corporate restructuring. The

Council, in the power of the Spirit, was and is a call to repentance, a call to conversion. From an over-centralized, over-papalized, over-monasticized, over-theologized Church, we have been summoned before the Gospels and the apostolic tradition. We have been called to conversion.

We, who have been more American and Catholic than Christian, have been called to conversion. *We, who came to listen to the orchestra, have been called to become the orchestra.*

Finally, what do we do about all this? There is no mystery here. There are no new, complicated programs to develop. We begin with ourselves. We acknowledge our resistances and we repent. We continue our own journeys of conversion. We stop compromising and avoiding and denying. We let ourselves die to all the personal and cultural biases that get in the way of the Gospel of Jesus Christ. Then we live it and preach it and teach it.

We meet together every week as a people. What's more, we have seasons, liturgical seasons. The wonderful rediscovery of the catechumenate has given Lent back to us—the real Lent, Lent as the final

87

approach to baptism and the renewal of baptism. Gabe Huck, of Chicago, puts this beautifully and powerfully:

> However many the exceptions of past and even of present, the church's direction is this: once a year we approach the waters to baptize. One night of all the nights in the cycle of seasons the waters are moved and the words of baptism are spoken. It was clearly so in our early times when being a Christian meant choosing an unusual way of life, one entered into only after a long time of testing. And slowly, perhaps because the times are not so different now, it again becomes clear that this is how we are to act.
>
> Once a year seems the right rhythm, or as close to it as we can get, for summoning catechumens to the font. Once a year is as often as we can put ourselves through this night for it takes many days to approach it, many days to get over it. The marvelous accidents of earth's place and sun's place, of axis and of orbit make cycles within human cycles so that days can be named and remembered, rhythms established. In our tradition, our way of being church, each one's baptism, while once for all life, remains the image of struggle and of dying and rising that fills a life. We have named a day in the year's cycle when we face those waters again. We work ourselves up to drawing other persons into those waters. Doing that, we have all we can take of baptism for a long time. We cannot more often than this have any candidate prepared. But even more, we cannot really be this serious and this beautiful and this painfully close to the waters more than once a year. (*The Three Days*, LTP.)

We have, then, what we need: the feasts, the cycles, the weekly meetings. There are, of course, other things that can help. We have alluded to them already: things like Bible-sharing groups, retreats, parish missions, RENEW. These things are more intense sometimes and may get us moving or over a hump. Only some make use of these special means, but that is all right: whatever anyone gains benefits us all.

We all have the feasts, the cycles, the weekly meetings. They can be perfunctory and totally lacking in power or they can be the source and summit of all that we are. In Romans 10: 14-17, Paul says:

> But how can they call to him for help if they have not believed? And how can they believe if they have not heard the message? And how can they hear if the message is not proclaimed? And how can the message be proclaimed if messengers are not sent out? As the scripture says, "How wonderful is the coming of messengers who bring good news." But not all have accepted the Good News. Isaiah himself said, "Lord, who believed our message?" So then, faith comes from hearing the message, and the message comes through preaching Christ.

"The Church in the past was renewed by saints."

Part Three

The Weekly Gathering

Liturgy of the Word

In Part One we reflected on sacrament and liturgy. Now I want to take a closer look at our weekly gathering: what we have, what we might do. I have the following questions in mind: What are we doing? Why are we doing it? Might we do something else?

It should become clear as we go along that what we have now is radically different from what we called "the Holy Sacrifice of the Mass." What we do have, radically different as it is, is a transition piece. The documents governing the liturgy are a jumble of new and old language, new and old image. What's more, the vernacular liturgies are translations from the Latin, so we have quite a way to go before the cultural transition is complete.

We begin at the beginning, the gathering itself.

Some years ago, I read a story about an alcoholic. It was a fairly typical story. A young man graduated from school, got a job, was married, had some children, bought a house. Along the way he started to drink. At some point the drinking took over. Eventually he lost his family and his job. He was one of the few who made it all the way to skid row. After many years of bumming around, he found himself one morning in a gutter.

As he described it, he woke up and suddenly, without knowing how, he felt that God was with him. He felt God say to him, "You don't have to be this way anymore. It's time to start a new life." He said,

> God touched me. I felt new. I used to be a Catholic, so I got cleaned up as best I could and started to look for a Catholic Church. It was Sunday morning. I was still dirty and I smelled of cheap wine, but I went to church. People were going in. When they saw me, they turned their eyes away and gave me a wide berth. It wasn't long before I realized that I really didn't belong there. Later on I tried another Catholic Church, and the same thing happened.
>
> That afternoon I was walking down the street when a guy pulled up next to me in his car and invited me in. He told me that I looked down on my luck and asked

me if I would like to go to an AA meeting. I said yes and off we went. I was about five feet inside the room of the meeting when someone came up to me, threw his arms around me and said, "Welcome home, brother."

Where were the Christians gathered?

John wrote: "How can we say we love God whom we don't see, if we don't love our neighbor whom we do see?" Jesus said: "By this shall all know that you are my disciples, that you love one another. . . . This is my commandment: Love one another as I have loved you."

How can we gather as a community of the disciples of Jesus without showing our love for each other? Jesus was explicit: "Not everyone who says, 'Lord, Lord' will enter the kingdom of God. Those who will be saved are those who hear the word of God and do it."

We are a worshipping community when we don't separate loving God from loving our neighbor. It is scandalous for Christians to gather while ignoring each other.

Catholic liturgy begins with the *Christian* gathering of the assembly. That is why the bishops at the Council could describe the liturgy as the "summit," the high point, the best expression of our being the body of Christ, the messianic presence. There are, no doubt, deeper, more powerful, better expressions of Christian discipleship from time to time. I think here of things like moments of difficult and generous forgiveness, of laying down our lives in martyrdom, of sharing with the poor. But the weekly gathering, week in and week out, is when we are the constantly recurring sign that we are a people who love each other.

This is why I quoted earlier from *Environment and Art in Catholic Worship*: "Among the symbols with which the liturgy deals, none is more important than the assembly of believers." *None.* What we do and how we do it makes liturgy (and everything else) sacrament—God acting in and through the material and the human.

In another place is the directive that when churches are renovated or new ones built, a special chapel should be built for the reservation of the Blessed Sacrament. The worship space of our Sunday liturgies should no longer contain a tabernacle! The new worship space of the new liturgy is to be made holy—a sanctuary—by the way in which we gather: "Where two or three of you gather in my name, I will be there in your midst." The altar rail has been removed.

What the reform of Vatican II wants us to discover is that Christ is present not only in the Blessed Sacrament but in the assembly. Nothing is taken away. We are still to discover Christ in the Eucharist, but *also* in the gathering, and in his word, in the silences and in the communion.

This strikes right at the root of God-me piety, of individualism, and of the need for conversion to community.

For many, this seems new. But it is not new at all. Some have said to me, "Father Lange, this is your idea of liturgy, but how about those of us who like to go to church to be quiet and say our prayers? That's the way we were brought up." It is not my idea or anyone's particular preference. It is the directive of the Church and it makes sense.

The way we gather, then, is itself sacramental. The gathering space becomes holy, Christ becomes present to us because we "gather in his name"; that is, we make an effort to love each other. Anyone who sees what we are doing should be able to say, "These people really care about each other."

Father Eugene Walsh taught liturgy at Catholic University in Washington for a number of years. His students were seminarians and others preparing for ministry. Today he is retired and spends his time writing and going around the country teaching what the Church is asking in the reform of the liturgy. His materials are clear, easy to read, and practical. Everyone involved in liturgy (therefore, everyone) should read them all. (They are available through Pastoral Arts Associates (PAA).)

Father Walsh suggests that "love" is a work that is too big for us to deal with. He suggests that we translate "love" as "hospitality" and "presence." Hospitality and presence are more manageable. We can imagine ourselves being hospitable and present to each other. What would our weekly gatherings look like if we come together this way?

We would see people greeting each other on the way into the building. Inside we would see people walking around and in little groups talking to each other. Some would already have taken their places but would still be engaged in conversation with those around them. Children would be searching out their friends, and the bum I described earlier would be made to feel at home.

That's what hospitality is about: making people feel welcome and at home. What a difference it makes when you go somewhere and meet someone whose face lights up and who says, "Good to see you! How are you doing?" It makes you feel good. It makes you feel cared for. Isn't that at least part of what loving is all about?

Being hospitable is easily enough managed. It doesn't mean that you have to take someone home with you or give them your car. It means that, right here, right now, I want to pay attention to you, welcome you, make you feel at home. If I have never met you, I introduce myself and let you know that I am glad you are here.

This is the way the community is formed as a worshipping community. Worship is loving God *and* our neighbor, not just in words, but in deed. Our hospitality to each other is the beginning of worship.

The one who presides, of course, must be in the middle of all this. He (in the current discipline) is the symbolic center of the community. He sets the tone, helps to create the atmosphere of worship. His hospitality, his warmth and welcome in the midst of his people, authorizes, encourages, and sets the example for them to do likewise.

Some may find this business of greeting each other difficult. It is not the way they were brought up. It is not what "going to church" means for them. That is why it is so important and so necessary to go to such great lengths to explain the reform, where it comes from, how radical the change is, and what high hopes the bishops have for it.

Jesus said that unless we take up our cross everyday and follow him, we cannot be his disciples. Greeting each other when we gather is sacrament in the basic meaning of that word: *to make holy*. It is in caring for each other that we make the assembly holy. It is this that makes sacrament, the ministry of the worshipping community.

All right, we have gathered in the Lord's name. At the appointed time we have our first hymn. It is a gathering hymn. In the midst of the noise and chatter of the assembling community, the music starts. We begin to sing together, to join our hearts and voices in praise and thanksgiving.

Then the one who presides leads us in the sign of the cross. We remember, not only the cross, but the Father and the Son and the Holy Spirit, in whose name we gather.

The presider greets the assembly: "The Lord be with you" or some variant. It is one of the four times that he does this. The meaning is: "You have gathered in his name. He is present. Pay attention." I always say something like: "We have greeted and welcomed each other. Now let us be quiet together and welcome the Lord whom we have invited by gathering in his name. The Lord is here." We then pause for a moment of silence.

The new liturgy does not do away with silence. As a matter of fact, it can't work without silence. The new liturgy creates periods of silence in the appropriate places in the rhythm of the liturgy. It is essential to stand together quietly to welcome the Lord who comes to be present in their midst.

The beginning of prayer is presence, paying attention. I don't think I am exaggerating by saying that many of our people do not know how to be quiet, to listen to their hearts. Even those who used to come to church to "say their prayers" did just that: they didn't come to listen, they came to talk.

If we are to pray the liturgy, we have to know this first step of prayer, to stand before God in silence, to let his presence touch us. We have to teach people how to use silence, how to be quiet. Let your heart be sensitive to the Lord's presence. Don't talk. Listen.

A lady once said to me, "When you first started this silence business, I wondered, 'What is he up to now?' I was fidgety and bothered that you took so long. Now I don't think you take long enough."

We can learn to be quiet together, to enter into prayer together. "The Lord be with you."

After the silence, so we can be attentive to God in whose presence we stand together, we may be invited to remember our sins or even confess our sinfulness together. Then the presider greets the Lord with "Lord, have mercy" or one of the variations. We respond, "Lord, have mercy." I believe that most liturgists would agree that this is simply a greeting. The Lord is present. We welcome him.

With our hearts focused on the present God, we pray the *Gloria*. Notice, please, that I say "pray," not "recite." We are not about the mindless business of recitation. We have entered the holy. If we have been paying attention to what we are doing, we are in awe. It is God to whom we speak: *We praise you. We bless you. We worship you. We give you thanks for your glory. . . . For you alone are the holy one. You alone are the Lord. You alone are the most High.*

Putting our awe into words of praise engages our minds and hearts and bodies more fully in what we came to do, to worship our God together. It is what Father Walsh calls the ministry of the worshipping community, to pay attention and respond.

101

Now the presider invites us to pray, to lift up to the Father whatever burdens we carry in our hearts. It is another dimension of worship, to trust in the Father's love, to confide in him, to believe that he wants to share our burdens. Of course, a considerable period of silence is required here so that we can do this. This quiet time is concluded with a prayer by the presider.

We sit down. Our minds and hearts are now ready to listen to God's word. The reader steps to the pulpit and proclaims that word. The first reading is a preparation for the Gospel. It comes from the Hebrew scriptures or from the Acts of the Apostles. It puts us in touch with the people who have gone before us, who themselves have struggled with what it means to have been called and chosen to be God's people. This is their story and our story. Something happened to them, and they tried to put it into words. We proclaim and listen to their words so that we can discover that experience in our lives.

God is present in his word. We experience that presence as we pay attention. We respond to the proclaiming of the word by saying "Thanks be to God." We can do that perfunctorily, mindlessly, or we can indeed be grateful both for having been able to be present when the word of God is proclaimed and for the word itself.

The second part of the response is silence. We do not just pass over this word of God. It isn't a commercial or empty chatter or even the poetry of a genius. It is God's word for us, here, now. We pause for a while. We listen to our hearts, where God speaks to us. Our heart's attitude is "God, what are you saying to me?"

The third part of the response is a psalm.

A second reading and quiet time follow. During our special seasons of Advent, Lent and Easter, this second reading is coordinated with the first as preparation for the Gospel. During the rest of the year, this second reading is an attempt to get us in touch with as much of the Bible as possible over a three-year cycle.

What we have been engaged in is the liturgy of *the Word*. It is a rhythm of paying attention to what is going on outside of ourselves and then paying attention to our hearts. All of it has been leading up to the Gospel and the homily. All of it is preparation to hear again the stories and sayings of Jesus. Jesus is *our* Lord, *our* Savior, God's *Word made flesh*. Jesus is the reason we are here. The deepest meaning of our lives is that we are his disciples. We have been baptized or are being prepared to be baptized into his death and resurrection. He lives in our hearts. We are filled with his Spirit.

The Gospel acclamation is intoned. We rise together as a posture of reverence. We resound to the acclamation. The verse is chanted. We respond again. Meanwhile, the one about to proclaim the Gospel bows low and prays, "Almighty God, cleanse my heart and my lips that I might worthily proclaim the Gospel."

He calls out to the assembly: "The Lord be with you." This is the second time it is said. Again, it means "The Lord is here. Pay attention. Open your hearts. The Lord is in the Gospel." He proclaims the Gospel, and we respond, "Praise to you, Lord Jesus Christ." He kisses the book saying silently, "May the words of the Gospel wipe away our sins."

The homily which follows is, more than anything else, a sharing of the preacher's faith and understanding. Those who preach pray over the word and study it until it is their own. For them it has become a prophetic word, a converting word, an inspiring word. This is their primary authority to preach. They are preaching, not their own ideas and feelings, but God's word as they have made it their own.

Silence follows the homily so that again we may attend to our hearts, where the Lord can speak to us.

We conclude the Liturgy of the Word by professing our faith together and then, through the General Intercessions, intercede for all humanity.

There is a rhythm to this Liturgy of the Word. It looks like this:

- Gathering—welcoming each other
- Song—coming together in our singing
- Silence—welcoming God
- Greeting and Praise—Lord, have mercy; Gloria
- Invitation to Prayer
- Silence—giving our burdens to God
- Reading I
- Silence
- Psalm
- Reading II
- Silence
- Gospel Acclamation

- Gospel
- Homily
- Silence
- Creed
- General Intercessions

The Liturgy of the Word builds to a climax, the Gospel of Jesus Christ. Together we come to stand before God, to open our hearts to his presence. We praise him, we unburden ourselves. We listen to a reading that sets the stage. And then the Gospel is proclaimed.

We have gathered to meet God. Everything we do in that gathering is subject to the basic question: Does it help us to experience God?

The silences are essential, which is why they are part of the General Norms for the Roman Missal. If the "silences" are no more than a pause, nothing will happen. If we take seriously what we are doing, then we will instruct the community often in the use of silence and make sure that our silences are long enough for something to happen.

Now, some comments:

(1) First of all, the rules and structures are the result of a period of experimentation after Vatican II. Our way of structuring the Liturgy of the Word is not the only way it can be structured. In other places and cultures it is structured differently. What we have since 1975 is a prayer structure that could be used as a personal prayer structure. Prayer requires that we disengage our minds and hearts from other things and pay attention to God's presence in us and around us.

Try it for yourself. Sing a hymn. Be quiet and welcome God, as he fills the space around you and fills your heart. Praise and thank him for a while. Lift up your burdens to him. Read something from scripture. Be quiet and listen to your heart. Read from the Gospel. Be quiet and listen.

Liturgy is a structure for prayer. As I have said before, this means that those responsible for liturgy, presiders and liturgy committees, must be people of prayer or they won't have any idea what they are about. They need to have experience in personal prayer and group prayer or they won't know how to use the structure to help the assembly experience God.

(2)   What is or is not emphasized has a lot to do with what is experienced as important, as well as what can be important. In the Liturgy of the Word, everything is leading up to the Gospel. I find the psalm response and the second reading (remember that this reading is not connected with the Gospel) to be distracting. The silence is a response, and the psalm seems like clutter. If it is sung (and not all the psalms were written as songs), it takes more time and emphasis than the Gospel. There are other opportunities to sing psalms. I experience it as a distraction. Do we jump into psalm singing because we don't appreciate or trust the silence?

I am coming at this from a particular point of view: what do we hope to get out of reading the word of God together? Don't we do it because we are disciples and have come together to struggle together with the word of the Master? I would much prefer to see a period of sharing after the silence rather than a psalm. Wouldn't it say something of what we were together for, and wouldn't it show the importance of the word for us, if we took a couple of minutes for people to share in response to questions like "What is God saying to you? What is God saying to us?"

I know that there are lots of explanations for the use of the psalm. I know that there are lots of people who have written on the value of praying the psalms. I said in the beginning that this book is personal and pastoral. I preside over the weekly gathering in our parish and I am interested in getting as much as we can out of the little time we have to struggle with God's word. We experience the psalm and the second reading as distracting. Please don't tell me that I haven't had good experiences with psalms. My point is that it doesn't fit and that, in both time and emphasis, it seems more important than the Gospel.

(3) Let's go back to the beginning. Another problem I have is with entrance processions. Again, it is a matter of emphasis. What are we saying by having an entrance procession? Who is processing and why? Doesn't the procession of ministers (including the presider) give the impression that here come the ones who count, or here come the ones who will perform? It is worse still when someone announces: "Let us stand and greet the celebrant, Father So-and-So." The

community celebrates. The presider presides over the celebration.

You see, what is going on here is one indication that we are in the early stages of developing an adequate structure for a worshipping community. We still have leftovers from when we gathered to be present at the priest's celebration. The language in the documents on the liturgy is littered with these inconsistencies.

(By now you have probably noticed that I am trying to have my cake and eat it, too. I am claiming obedience to the norms for what I am saying and, at the same time, criticizing these norms. I know I'm doing that, so I'll explain why I can. There are obviously more important and less important principles and guidelines. There are some things which describe the new vision and there are leftovers from the old. What I have been doing (and will continue to do) is point out the problems and inconsistencies of the less important with the more basic.)

(4)   Another problem I have is with people wearing robes. I find that odd. Father Eugene Walsh makes a strong case for eliminating the robes. He argues from the meaning of a community at worship. The wor-

shipping community not only gathers, listens and responds, but some among them lead the song, proclaim the word, serve and minister the Eucharist. He argues that those with special ministries should sit with the assembly, come forth to minister and then return to their places in the assembly. Rather than special robes and a place in a procession, which symbolize a special group, this coming from and returning to the assembly says that what goes on here is the work of the assembly, presided over by the presider.

Let's reflect on this for a moment. It touches on all that we do. Many of the ways we behave carry a second message besides the obvious one. Have you ever been cut off when trying to explain something? The obvious thing that happened is that you were cut off. It probably has happened to you many times. Those who cut you off clearly thought they had something to say, but they also communicated that they didn't think what you had to say was worth listening to.

Some years ago, a very upset young lady came to see me. A couple of nights earlier she had been out with some friends and brought them all back to her apartment as a surprise party for her husband of a few months. Now, this young man was going to college and had informed his wife that he had a lot of work to do the week of his birthday. Several times he had told her he wanted to wait till later to celebrate his birthday. Yet she came bursting in with a bunch of people to surprise him—and he became furious. The obvious thing she did was throw a party. The non-verbal, symbolic message that he got was: "You asked me not to do this, but I don't care at all about what you want. I'm throwing this party to make myself feel good."

Processions and robes say something else besides just being processions and robes. So also does a community at worship in which ministers come forth from and return to the assembly.

(5) Another thing I would like to comment on is what happens after we have gathered and been reminded that God is present—"The Lord be with you." There are options. One option is sprinkling, a renewal of baptism. Wonderful! We are reminded that we have died with Christ and risen with him to a new life, that we have been filled with the Holy Spirit. Notice that this is not the same thing as blessing ourselves with holy water as we enter. In this sprinkling

we stand together, a people made one precisely through baptism—one baptism, one faith, one Spirit, one God, one people. Wonderful!

A second option is the penitential rite, which may include the "I confess." As with everything else, presumably we do it because it is worth doing. We expect it to mean something, to accomplish something. The presider says some variation of "Let's call to mind our sins."

The question is what is supposed to be happening here? Is this an abbreviated form of the sacrament of reconciliation? Should we be examining our consciences? I don't think so. What is going on here is part of the flow of the prayer that we have begun. We have just been invited to pay attention to God's presence with us. If, in fact, we come before God, if we consciously enter his presence and let his presence reach our minds and hearts, then we do not even need a reminder that we are sinful. We know it. To enter the sacred, to really encounter the Holy, reveals us to ourselves as nothing and as sinful. It is part of the experience of the holy, of God. We encounter the creator and we know our creatureliness.

113

This is a completely different thing from a modesty about our accomplishments or a morbid self-depreciation. What happens here happens only when we come before God, and we cannot know it any other way. We enter the light and we know our darkness, our nothingness, our sin. We come before Truth and we know what in us is false, in our thoughts and in our words, in what we have done and what we have failed to do. The awareness is not so much of specific sins as of creatureliness, nothingness, sinfulness. This is the real meaning of humility.

And because we have come before the God revealed by Jesus, we have come before God who is love. In that light we are liberated instead of being crushed. We are free! We do not have to pretend that we are great and wonderful and sinless. We are loved just as we are. We are forgiven and cherished.

This entering into the holy, into the presence of God who is with us and for us, is the penitential rite. It is, in fact, the beginning of all real prayer. It is what we gather for. It is the condition for everything else that follows. It requires silence and attention. This is reverence.

(6)   If we have entered into the rhythm of prayer, we will be ready to hear the word of God. Perhaps not quite ready. For many Catholics, the Bible is a closed book, literally and figuratively. It is a mystery. The readings are not familiar or, even if familiar, not understood. The stories and prophetic words are about someone else long ago. They have nothing to do with now. Often enough, people simply endure the readings that are supposed to be life-giving.

It is a striking sign of life and hope for the American Church that all over the country there is a great deal of interest in the Bible among Catholics today. It is just a beginning, but it is there. If the Liturgy of the Word is to be life-giving, Bible sharing and study have to become part of the taken-for-granted way of life for us. And, week by week, year by year, we must be able to do something more with it at our weekly gatherings, and do a better job of introducing the Bible to our young in religious education programs.

At any rate, in our liturgies we listen to the word with a question in our hearts: "Lord, what do you want to say to me today?" We continue to listen to our hearts through the silence. Somewhere, maybe just one

115

word will stand out and speak to us. We may have heard it a hundred times before, but this time it has special meaning for us. So we pay attention to it. We struggle with it.

(7) The Gospel procession. All of the Liturgy of the Word has been building to the proclamation of the stories and sayings of Jesus, the Gospel. Once again, there is that zone of meaning around what we do that speaks, that teaches. In earlier times there was a grand procession that preceded the proclamation of the Gospel. There were candles and incense and elaborately sung Alleluias. Judging by the length of the Alleluias in the Latin *Liber Usualis,* the procession was quite long. Historically, this form of Gregorian chant was preceded by spontaneous jubilation, often mixed with singing in tongues.

The point is that this is the Good News of Jesus the Christ. He is the reason we gather. We are his disciples. He is the center of our lives.

I have yet to see, anywhere in the country, a movement to the Gospel that really speaks of its importance to us—a movement, a procession with dignity and solemnity and reverence and joy. What a different message we would get if we spent all the time and emphasis on a Gospel procession that we now spend on the responsorial psalm. If I might offer a homely analogy, it seems that what we are doing is offering lobster salad as an appetizer and hot dogs for the main course.

(8) Preachers. The General Instructions indicate that the homily should ordinarily be given by the priest. An interesting exception to that occurs in the Directory for Masses for Children, where it says, "With the consent of the pastor or rector of the church, one of the adults may speak to the children after the Gospel, especially if the priest finds it difficult to adapt himself to the mentality of children." And, later, "Even in Masses with children, attention is to be paid to the diversity of ministries so that Mass may stand out clearly as the celebration of a community."

I have two problems here. One is a matter of consistency and the other, far more basic, a matter of fighting God. The consistency issue is plain enough. Some priests (and I include myself here) don't know how to preach to children. Those who make the rules and know that it is important to help the children understand, say, "O.K., let a lay person do it who knows how and who is approved."

It is pretty clear that some priests don't really know how to preach to adults either. Why not allow them to designate a lay person who can? Not only would the priest no longer have to feel incompetent and guilty, he would also feel good that he was providing helpful homilies for his people.

The point, to be explicit, is if lack of competence is a reason for finding a substitute in one case, why can't substitutes be found in other cases where it would benefit everyone?

The most serious problem is the exclusionary legislation. The new liturgy is the work of the community. The literature makes this point often enough and emphatically enough. Paul speaks of the Church as the body of Christ which the Spirit gifts with apostles, prophets, preachers and teachers—among others, as we have said before. Preaching in the Church is a gift and ministry of the Holy Spirit. All over this country, at Cursillos, charismatic meetings, retreats and parish celebrations, I have experienced hundreds of lay people with the gift of preaching. When they preach, people are moved. (And the real sign that preaching and teaching are gifts of the Spirit is when people go away talking, not about the speaker, but about Christ.)

We are truly at the beginning of the renewal of Vatican II. This area is one of the leftovers. The Vatican II documents, the Synod of 1970, and so many other documents make it clear that Paul's vision of the Church is to be taken seriously, that the Spirit gifts the Church with ministries to grow in Christ. Those in authority are directed to help the laity discover and use their gifts. Then we run into this exclusion. Why is this territory staked out? Is this what God wants?

I am reminded how furious Jesus was with the Scribes and the Pharisees. He said that they thwarted God's desire by their own rules.

(9) More on preaching. The Liturgy of the Word is a ministry of the word. We don't proclaim it just for the sake of proclaiming, any more than we celebrate just for the sake of celebrating. Some liturgists hate to hear the words *teaching* and *liturgy* in the same sentence. I find that not only puzzling but incomprehensible. Not only do the documents speak of the cate-

119

chetical and teaching dimensions of liturgy, but any discussions of symbol, gesture or environment necessarily concerns itself with what is being communicated—that is, taught.

We are a cynical society when it comes to words. We don't pay much attention to them, even when we claim they are from God. It is the word-made-flesh that touches us, the word that is lived, not merely the word in a book.

Besides readers who struggle with the word before they read it in the liturgy, besides preachers who speak from their own attempts to live the word, we have two wonderful resources that we rarely experience. We have elders and beginners.

Efforts are made from time to time to allow others to speak in the assembly, but it is always done with an eye on avoiding conflict with the priest-preacher. I've heard talks given before the liturgy and after communion. They don't belong in either place. The word of sharing belongs as a response to the Gospel.

We need to hear from the elders of our communities. They are essential to a Church that grows Christians.

Elders are those who have lived the Gospel, whose lives have been transformed by Christ. They are people who have been set free from selfishness and greed, from fear and illusions, from the need to control and the need to please. They are not people who need to be sure. They live easily with the ambiguities of life. Jesus is the most important person in their lives. They live by the power of the Spirit. They are people who have struggled with the Gospel and made it their own. They don't need to quote it. They live it. One finds in them strength and compassion, joy and hope, gratitude and love.

Their lives are the Good News—and not just the consolation of the Gospel, but its challenge. They are not finished, and no one knows that better than they do. They are personalities. They are themselves. They are alive.

Elders are like guides up a mountain. They are there ahead of us showing us it can be done. The rest of us are strung out behind them. Without them we wander around the valley, not quite believing we can make it up the mountain.

Elders do not teach by quoting other teachers. They teach with authority, because they are close to the author. They teach from what they have experienced. When we experience them, we sense something missing in ourselves. In the early Church, elders were the leaders of the Christian communities.

Another group we need to hear from are the newly converted. The RCIA provides a few opportunities for that, but it isn't enough. We need their vitality. In them we encounter the challenge to be converted again ourselves. We see them doing it, seeking Jesus at the center of their lives, opening themselves to the power of the Spirit. We are reminded of the joy of conversion, of letting go of the old self and of becoming new in Christ. We are reminded that following Christ is a continuous dying and rising, never finished. Those of us who have come a little way know that these new converts have only just begun. We know that their new life in Christ is fragile, not yet deeply rooted, not yet deeply suffered through. At the same time, we know our bondedness with them. We gain new life from them, and they receive support from us.

What good are elders, though, if there is no opportunity to hear from them? How do we receive new life from converts if their journey is not shared with us?

Sometimes a simple witness is better than a homily. Sometimes a witness would follow a homily. There is great power here.

(10) The selection of readings. I know that a great deal of work went into the selection of readings for our current three-year cycle. I know the rhythm of the seasons and realize that the readings chosen for these seasons are designed to focus our attention on particular aspects of our journey in Christ. Therefore, we have the seasons of Advent, Lent and Easter. That leaves us with the rest of the year as Ordinary Time.

Why not have special periods in Ordinary Time available for special areas of concern? During those times, special readings could be selected that ground special teaching.

The North American Forum on the Catechumenate and some liturgists have elevated the current selection

123

of readings in the Lectionary almost to the point of making fidelity to it the touchstone of orthodoxy. I am not suggesting anarchy with regard to the Sunday readings, as there simply must be some discipline about these things. On the other hand, it seems to me that there are some compelling reasons for a bishop to authorize an approved "package" of teachings with readings for particular communities for a particular set of Sundays in Ordinary Time. The decision would be pastoral. It is difficult to separate the pastoral role from the teaching role. Jesus was the good shepherd and, of course, a lot of what he did was teach.

There are a lot of topics about which our people are confused: love, sexuality, wealth and simplicity, justice, community, healing, prayer, the Holy Spirit. And how about the bishops' teachings on peace and justice and on the economy? How about the pope's teachings? If these things are so important, why are they not included somehow when we gather to be formed by God's word? Most of Paul's letters were written to be read by the local community in response to present community problems. It was a way of bringing the community to grips with how their faith should be lived.

What I am suggesting is that at times the pastoral leadership of a parish might come to the conclusion that the community needs to hear some clear teaching about a particular area of Christian life. I am speaking here as a simple parish priest who is frustrated. I know my people need instruction in a number of areas and I know that relatively few would turn out for special instruction. I know it has been suggested that you should decide on what you want to teach, and then look over the Lectionary readings to see how you can use them as a springboard for that teaching. I've done it myself, but it's not doing the best we can or the best that our people deserve. At times a series of teachings could be drawn up and submitted to the bishop for approval. It would mean an occasional and temporary interruption in Ordinary Time.

I come back to a very basic question: What is the weekly gathering for? Is it just to make us feel spiritual? Feel good? Is that what true worship is about?

Most of what I have said so far is pretty tame. Many of us get by with talking Church and prayer and spirituality and liturgy. That's safe. Jesus would never have been crucified if that had been all he talked about and did.

The question is why do we gather each week as the disciples of Jesus? In the words of the Council, we gather to be "set on fire." For what? To bring about the reign of God. If we are going to do that in any responsible way, then we've got to talk about our needs and questions in the here and now.

We have workshops and conferences for religious and clergy. We wouldn't dream that we could deal adequately with some issues with the clergy in one twenty-minute homily. Why can't we give our people in the parishes some in-depth blocks of time at our weekly meetings?

It seems to me that the greatest obstacle to using the Liturgy of the Word in a really effective way is a leftover from the pre-Council days of "going to Mass to watch the priest perform." We have restored the Liturgy of the Word, but we are only now coming to grips with how it can be used. Those who would idolize the Lectionary have not yet been liberated from the "going to Mass" mentality.

All of this is related to a final comment on the teaching dimension of our weekly gathering.

(11) Teaching. I have said repeatedly that what we are concerned about shows up in what we talk about, what we do, and how we do it. Somehow we are supposed to be a people, the people of God, who know that we are a people about the business of bringing about the reign of God. How can we get the idea that Christianity is about repentance and growth and continual conversion unless it is preached and witnessed to?

What does it teach us when we come together and see that no one speaks to anyone else? What does it teach us about discipleship when no one we know ever talks about it? What do we teach others, and what do they teach us, when no one is ever seen taking time out to pray or read the Bible? How are we supposed to understand that Christian discipleship involves being concerned about the poor and homeless and hurting if we ourselves don't show concern and don't see others doing so?

There are issues about the quality of life all around us—local, state, national, and international. When are they brought up? How are we involved individually and as a people in things like libraries and school boards, health care facilities, programs for legislation, shelter, and so forth? What does it teach us when these things are absent from the Liturgy of the Word, from bulletins and committees and witness?

Again, and I say this with great pain and frustration, what do we learn of Christian discipleship from a Church that maintains decision-making structures which exclude the laity? What do we learn from a Church that perpetuates patriarchy and refuses to acknowledge full discipleship of women? What are we supposed to learn from a Church that prefers sexism and celibacy to Eucharist?

Let us make no mistake about it. We can have all the catechisms and Bibles and teachings from on high, but in the end they say nothing and do nothing. The only word that teaches and converts is the living word: what we do.

Part Four
Liturgy of the Eucharist

Eucharist is an action, something we do together. We—the disciples of Jesus, united in the Spirit with each other and with all that is—we gather around the table to offer praise and thanksgiving to the Father, to remember, and to share the bread and cup, renewing the covenant of forgiveness and unity. Christ, already present in the gathering and in the word, becomes present in a new way as we do this. At the same time, we are joined in him to all those around the world and down the centuries who have shared in this bread and cup, who are part of the body of Christ with us, and who have lived to bring about the reign of God.

Eucharist in the beginning was simple. At the last meal Jesus would share with his friends before his death, he took bread, broke it, told them it was his body and give it to them to eat. At the end of the supper he took a cup filled with wine, told them it was his blood and the blood of a new covenant. He gave it to them and they drank. He asked them to do this as a memorial.

A memorial is different from an anniversary. A memorial is something that, once begun, is continued. The passover meal of the Jews is a memorial. It begins with retelling the story of their liberation from slavery in Egypt; and it begins, not by saying "Once *they* were slaves," but by saying "Once *we* were slaves." What began then continues now. The struggle for liberation goes on, and we are part of it. So with the memorial of Eucharist, the covenant sealed in the blood of Christ is entered into by all those who share in the bread and the cup. Paul would say that, because we share the one loaf, we are one body in Christ.

The covenant we share is given by God through Christ. We agree to the covenant by eating the bread and drinking from the cup. And the covenant is for the forgiveness of sins. It is a covenant of reconciliation: God will dwell in our hearts; the Spirit will fill us and make us one with God and each other.

The eating of the bread, then, is much more than I was asked to believe before I received my first communion. Then, I was expected to know only that the communion wafer was the body of Christ. The act of taking and eating is a renewal of the covenant of baptism. It is reconciliation and forgiveness accepted. It is the renewal of the commitment to discipleship.

The act of communion is a joining of myself to the body of Christ, and that body of Christ is Christ as head and we as members. I acknowledge my communion, not only with God, but with all who have been baptized into Christ.

Eucharist in the beginning was simple. Christians gathered in each other's homes for the "breaking of the bread," a memorial of the Lord's sharing of his body and blood. Very early on, in Jewish fashion, the meal was preceded by a prayer of thanksgiving. Since the Greek word for thanksgiving is *eucharist,* the gathering for the meal became "Eucharist."

From the beginning there was a link between this meal and the death of Jesus. As Paul describes it (I Cor. 11:23-26), Jesus said: "This is my body, which is for

131

you. . . . This cup is the new covenant in my blood."
Then Paul adds: "Whenever you eat this bread and
drink this cup, you are proclaiming the Lord's death
until he comes." The death of Jesus was the symbol
of the unlimited, unconditional love of the Father.
There was nothing more to give. Sharing in
Eucharist, in communion, is remembering his giving
up his body for us, the spilling of his blood to seal the
new covenant.

Now, the meaning of Jesus, the Word made Flesh,
the sacrament of God, his life, teaching, death, resurrection, sending of the Spirit — all this cannot be re-
duced to one word or phrase. This is the mystery of
God-with-us. Each of the Gospels gives a different
meaning to Christ. And Paul speaks of the death of
Jesus as redemption, reconciliation, expiation. The
letter to the Hebrews describes the death of Jesus as a
"sacrifice" and Jesus as the "eternal high priest."

The name "priest" was given *only* to Jesus for the first
several hundred years of the Church. We were called
a "priestly people" because we are joined to Christ.
The one who presided over Eucharist was an elder or
prophet, eventually a bishop or presbyter. As people

reflected on the connection between the death of Jesus, the sacrifice of himself, and the Eucharistic meal, they began to speak of Eucharist as sacrifice. It was a short step from there to naming the one who presided over the sacrifice a "priest." Then, too, the table became an altar. When this first began to happen, St. Augustine roundly condemned it and called it heresy. Only Jesus is priest, he said, and we, joined to him, are all together a priestly people.

But the language of sacrifice and priesthood prevailed. Over the centuries, the priestly class developed more and more elaborate rituals, and the simple symbolism of a meal was practically lost.

In the beginning there was a simple sharing of the bread and cup with thanksgiving. It was a meal charged with remembrance and significance, and they recognized him in the breaking of the bread.

The liturgical reform of Vatican II makes the following decrees: "The Order of the Mass is to be revised in a way that will bring out more clearly the intrinsic nature and purpose of its several parts. . . . For this purpose the rites are to be simplified, due course being taken to preserve their substance." And, a little earlier: "In this reform both texts and rites should be so drawn up that they express clearly the holy things they signify and that the Christian people, as far as possible, are able to understand them with ease."

It seems to me we have a way to go before we easily experience ourselves as the friends of Jesus gathered around the table to break the bread and share the cup of our covenant meal, while giving praise and thanksgiving to our Father.

The Latin Mass of the Council of Trent was the work of the priest, but the liturgy of Vatican II is the work of the assembled community. The Latin Mass was said at the altar in a sanctuary fenced off by an altar rail. The Vatican II liturgy is celebrated around a table (there is no altar rail). The radical newness of the Vatican II Eucharistic liturgy has to do with the recovery of the description of Eucharist as, not only meal, but covenant meal.

The structure of the Liturgy of the Eucharist is simple: (1) preparation of the table, (2) Eucharistic prayer, (3) communion, (4) concluding rite. Another way of describing it would be (1) setting the table, (2) prayer before the meal, (3) covenant meal, (4) concluding rite.

The first part is a preparing of the table. Remember that we have just finished the Liturgy of the Word, climaxing in the Gospel and the homily. We have built up to a high point and opened our hearts to the word. Now it is time to rest for a few minutes. I think the most appropriate thing to do here is to be quiet. We have heard the word. Now we need to struggle with it, and for that we need silence. We listen with our hearts to the question: *Lord, what are you saying to me today?* The quality of this silence, this reverence for the word, is often enhanced by some soft instrumental music.

How important this silence is, this time of response to the word! Some presiders sit down after the homily for a period of quiet. That can be done, but we still have the down time of the preparation of the table. For me, it is matter of pace. The time of response is important. Catechumens are dismissed after the Liturgy of the Word to go off with a catechist in order to continue their reflection on the word. How I wish we could do all that before going on to the Eucharist! We could split up into small groups, struggling with questions like "What did it say? What did it mean? What will it cost?" What a difference it would make! What a sacrament it would be — disciples being disciples, wrestling with the teaching of the Master, being formed by it!

This is something that people do sometimes on retreats or special gatherings as they discover the power of God's word. This brings up again the question: *Why do people have to go away from our parishes to find these opportunities?*

I prefer quiet (perhaps with soft music) during the preparation of the gifts. This, of course, is not an "offertory." We are simply preparing the table. It should be done simply. The bread and cup are brought to the table by members of the community — and this presents problems. There is motion here, and some people seize on that to develop pageantry. There are ordinary times and there are festive times, so if we make ordinary times elaborate there is no way to be festive. And what is appropriate for Sunday is not necessary during the week. Furthermore, what is

136

good for a small gathering is not necessarily good for a large one.

Still, good symbols and pageantry are important. They help to set the mood. I remember some special meals. The table was already set. The family would gather for Thanksgiving in our dining room with the exciting procession of food from the kitchen until finally it was capped off with a large golden-brown turkey. I've seen a similar elegance at restaurants where chateaubriand, or flaming steak, was served at the table.

A procession can be simple and dignified, but it should be symbolic: a nice decanter of wine, real bread. Perhaps, too, a hymn could be sung during the procession and the final preparations of the table.

When the table is ready, the presider once again reminds us that the Lord is present: "The Lord be with you." This is the third time we hear that reminder. The Lord is present in the praise and thanksgiving (Eucharist), in the remembering and in the meal. Then we are exhorted to lift up our hearts. We respond by saying, "Yes, we will pay attention with our hearts; yes, we lift up our hearts to the Lord." Then

137

comes the invitation: "Let us give thanks to the Lord, our God," to which we respond: "It is right to give him thanks and praise."

The opening words of this prayer of praise and thanksgiving are always some variation of "Father, all-powerful and ever-living God, we do well always and everywhere to give you thanks."

The Eucharistic prayer is a prayer—something to be prayed, not simply recited. In the days of the Latin Mass I personally knew priests who did not understand the Latin and who simply recited, pronounced, the words. Now the Eucharistic prayer is clearly a prayer, and prayer is work. It requires knowing to whom I address these words of praise and thanksgiving. It requires paying attention to what I am saying. It requires meaning sincerely what I say.

What's more, this is the prayer of the whole assembly: "Lift up your hearts. Let *us* give thanks to the Lord, our God." It is more clearly a prayer of the community in the Eucharistic prayers for children, where there are more acclamations and responses. It is not simply a prayer which the priest recites. It is a prayer led by the presider which all of us enter into.

138

This is a prayer of praise and thanksgiving (Eucharist). It has been known as such from very early on. Like all sacramental rituals, it is meant to sum up and express what we already are, what we do all the time. *We do well always and everywhere to give you thanks.*

Have you ever searched for a greeting card that would say just what you wanted to say, whose words would be your own words? Sometimes you find a prayer or a psalm that puts into words what you feel in your heart. When we read the Bible or the prayers of our liturgies, we are doing just about the reverse. Instead of finding something that says what we want to say, these prayers teach us or remind us what we ought to feel in our hearts. Others before us have experienced something and tried to put it into words. Our task is to rediscover the experience from their words, to make their words our words.

The liturgical prayer of Eucharist is a prayer of thanksgiving and praise. We are reminded that it is good always and everywhere to give thanks. Christian people are a grateful people, not occasionally, but always and everywhere.

139

The Christian assembly can never know the power of Eucharist until its people are always and everywhere, day in and day out, giving thanks to God. Unless the ritual is summing up what we live, the ritual is empty and borders on superstition: say the words and something magical will happen.

After close to forty years in the religious life and the priesthood, I am convinced that nothing is more powerful and effective in nourishing the life in the Spirit than a simple thank-you prayer. Paul tells us over and over that we become entirely new in Christ, that we no longer see the world or God or ourselves as pagans do. Nothing I know of works better to bring us the mind and heart of Christ than simple thank-you prayer. Nothing I know of brings our Eucharistic prayer alive and fresh like daily thank-you prayer.

Those responsible for liturgy should find such prayer easy enough to teach. Suggest the following: First, take ten straight minutes and do nothing but thank God for the good in your life. Do this in the morning and in the evening—just find ten minutes by yourself and go through a litany of thanksgiving.

140

Begin by remembering that you are talking to God (or Jesus or whatever name you use). Then begin your thanks. It might go like this: *Thank you, Jesus, for a new day. Thank you for a good night's sleep. Thank you for my wife (husband, parent, friend, child).*

When one item occurs to you, let it expand: "Thank you for my wife. Thank you for her love for me. Thank you for her patience," and so on.

Go through the past years. Remember those who have taught you, challenged you, gifted you. Look at the world around you. *Give thanks.*

The second thing to try is to offer thanks all day long. Look for things and people to give thanks for. Do it quietly, to yourself.

Being a grateful people is what makes the Eucharist our prayer. We are at the heart of the matter of the Eucharist and, even more deeply, of growing into real disciples of Jesus.

Jesus asks us to let God love us and forgive us. For that to really happen, we have to go further and actually trust God. That was the example given by the life

141

and teaching of Jesus—Jesus in the desert, Jesus at prayer, Jesus following the leading of the Spirit, Jesus yielding to his passion and death.

Trusting God and his love for us is not easy. Oh, it is easy enough to say the words, but it is quite another thing to stake our lives on it, to seek first the reign of God, to die to ourselves so that we may rise in the newness of the Spirit.

Unless we are hopelessly naive, trusting another in any serious way requires intimacy and repeated experiences of trustworthiness. It is not a question of whether or not the other person (or God) is in fact trustworthy. It is a question of our willingness to believe in that trustworthiness. Through time and repeated experience we see the other coming through, being there for us. That is how trust grows in us.

The more we remember, notice, acknowledge that God is with us and for us and generous, the more we grow in trust and the more we are willing to entrust our lives to him. Part of the genius of Hebrew prayer is that it almost always begins by remembering: *O, Lord, it was you who delivered us from slavery in Egypt* . . . Thanksgiving prayer enables us to grow in love and trust of God. Eucharist becomes our own prayer.

Recently, I have been reading *Sadhana - A Way to God* by Anthony de Mello, S.J., one of the most respected teachers of prayer of our time. After describing all sorts of prayer styles he writes:

> If I had to choose the one form of prayer that has made the presence of Christ most real in my life and given me the deepest sense of being supported and surrounded by the loving providence of God, I would unhesitatingly choose this, the last form of prayer I propose in this book, the Prayer of Praise. I would also choose it for the great peace and joy it has so often brought me in times of distress. The prayer consists, quite simply, of praising and thanking God for everything.

In our Eucharistic assembly we have begun to pray with thanksgiving, and are invited to join the angels and saints in praising God as we say, "Holy, holy, holy . . ." This is the cry of the seraphim in chapter six of Isaiah. It was the powerful visionary experience that turned Isaiah into a prophet:

> In the year King Uzziah died, I saw the Lord seated on a high and lofty throne, with the train of his garment filling the temple. Seraphim were stationed above: each of them had six wings: with two they veiled their faces, with two they veiled their feet, and with two they hovered aloft. "Holy, holy, holy is the Lord of hosts!" they cried one to the other. "All the earth is

143

filled with his glory!" At the sound of that cry, the frame of the door shook and the house was filled with smoke. Then I said, "Woe is me. I am doomed! For I am a man of unclean lips, living among a people of unclean lips; yet my eyes have seen the King, the Lord of hosts!"

This experience of God was overwhelming to Isaiah because to experience God is to know awe. In the presence of God one knows oneself as sinful and as nothing.

The word *holy* in Hebrew originally meant the "godliness of God." God is God, the all-mighty, the Creator, the inexpressible, the tremendous mystery. The "holy, holy, holy" of the angels means *God is God, God is God, God is God.*

Our Eucharistic prayer begins "All-mighty and ever-living God . . . "; and our initial response is "Holy, holy . . . , you are God, you are truly God." It focuses our attention on what we are really doing: we dare to come before God. We offer God our thanksgiving and praise. We remember his mighty deeds in our midst.

In Eucharistic Prayer II the presider continues: "Lord, you are holy indeed," emphasizing *Yes, you are God.*

Then he says: you are "the fountain of all holiness." We acknowledge that God shares his life, his godliness, his Spirit, his holiness with us. That is why we are called "the saints," "the holy ones," "the body of Christ." *We share in the exchange of divine life.*

It is this sharing in God's holiness, his Spirit, that makes us his people. It is gift. He is the fountain, the source.

Next comes the first invocation of the Spirit: "Let your Spirit come upon *these* gifts to make *them* holy, so that they may become for *us* the body and blood of our Lord, Jesus Christ." All that happens in the kingdom of God comes in and through the power of the Spirit. Jesus was conceived of the Holy Spirit, was filled with the Spirit at the baptism by John, and carried on his own work in the power of the Spirit. The new and last times begun in Jesus continued with Pentecost and are passed on to us at baptism when we receive the same Spirit. Now we pray that this Spirit will transform this bread and this wine on this table into the body and blood of Christ for *us* as *we* invoke the Spirit, remembering to give thanks and renew the covenant in his blood by breaking the bread and sharing the cup together. As the presider invokes the Holy Spirit, he extends his hands over the gifts in an ancient form of blessing.

In the narrative of institution, we are remembering in the midst of our prayer of thanksgiving: *Father, the main reason we give you thanks right now is because, on the night before he died, Jesus gave us this bread to be his body for us and this cup to be his blood of the new covenant for the forgiveness of sins.* This is the memorial, the remembering and entering into what began at the Last Supper.

It is inappropriate to call this remembering a "consecration." "Consecration" means "making holy"—the bread and cup become holy for us, the body and blood of Christ for us, in the course of a prayer of thanksgiving, invoking the Holy Spirit, remembering, calling on the Spirit again, making petitions, and sharing together this covenant meal. It is the whole action, the whole thing together that consecrates.

I find it equally inappropriate to be ringing bells during the narrative of remembering, as though only at this moment has Christ come among us. We might just as well ring bells as we gather and at the proclamation of the word.

So, we have remembered that Jesus gave us this bread to be his body and this cup of the new covenant. The presider then invites us to acclaim the memorial, and we respond: "Christ has died. Christ is risen. Christ will come again."

As we continue our prayer of thanksgiving, we say: "In memory of his death and resurrection, we offer you, Father, this life-giving bread, this saving cup. We thank you for counting us worthy to stand in your presence and serve you." *(Don't you find it odd that the prayer expects us to be standing? Every other time we are invited to pray, we stand. This is our usual posture of prayer. Yet right in the middle of this prayer, we kneel down. It is a leftover.)*

There are many paths to God. We are the people who remember Jesus as the way, especially in his dying and rising. In this memory we offer the bread and the cup. We thank the Father for counting us worthy to stand in his presence, not because we are good or have made ourselves worthy, but because he has made us worthy. This is the meaning of his justice.

147

He justifies us by his forgiveness and because he is the fountain of all holiness. We are reminded, too, that we have been called, chosen, and empowered to serve, to continue the work of Christ, to bring about the reign of God.

After we have prayed that the Spirit will transform the bread and cup into the body and blood of Christ, we call upon the Spirit to transform *us* into the body of Christ: "May all of us who share in the body and blood of Christ be brought together in unity by the Holy Spirit." Or, from Eucharistic Prayer III: "Grant that we who are nourished by his body and blood may be filled with his Holy Spirit and become one body, one Spirit in Christ."

We really need to notice the intent of this prayer. Because, among other things, we have been so taken up with the Real Presence in the Eucharist, we have neglected these invocations of the Holy Spirit and missed this reconsecration of ourselves. We have died and risen with Christ through baptism and have become his body. We, too, are filled with the Holy Spirit.

The Eucharistic prayers proceed in a simple way from the second invocation of the Spirit. We pray for the whole people of God, our leaders, those who have died, and, finally, ourselves.

We conclude our Eucharist (thanksgiving) to the Father: "Through him [Christ], with him, in him" — *our way to the Father is Christ* — "in the unity of the Holy Spirit [our unity], all glory and honor is yours, almighty Father, forever and ever." To which we respond, "Amen." Yes. So be it.

Having offered our prayer before the meal, we proceed to the meal itself. The rite is straightforward. Formed by God's work and filled with the Spirit, we dare to call God "Father" as Jesus did, and we pray as Jesus taught us. The presider expands on the petition "deliver us from evil," and then reminds us of the peace that Jesus promised, the peace to which we are called. Then we are invited to share a sign of peace with each other.

The sign of peace is not a greeting. We have already done that when we first began to gather. This is a sign that we are disciples of Jesus. We are a people

149

of peace, peacemakers. Because it is a sign (and not a greeting), it need be made only once, though some like to make it to more than one person.

This is another example of an element of our ritual which is of profound importance and whose significance is often missed entirely. When we have not greeted each other on arrival, when we have not gathered in the Lord's name, caring for each other, then this sign of peace is turned into a greeting and there is no real meaning. Jesus told his disciples that if they came to the altar to offer sacrifice and remembered that someone had something against them, they should first go and be reconciled and then come to the altar. These words of Jesus echo the Hebrew prophets, who say "Thus says the Lord: 'Away with your noisy sacrifices and cereal offerings. What I want,' says the Lord, 'are mercy and justice.' "

This sign of peace before communion is a sign to myself and to those around me that I am ready to renew the covenant of peace before God, that I have come to this moment bearing no grudges, carrying no resentment or bitterness, that I have settled my problems with others the best I can.

To make this sign sincerely is a challenge. If we took it seriously, knowing the judgment this sign is for us, would we not make the effort to be reconciled with everyone before we came together? We do, perhaps, think of the prescribed fast before communion, and we may say to ourselves, "I ate too late, so I can't go to communion." Yet we may fail to look inside, to examine our own relationships.

Jesus complained that the Scribes and the Pharisees strained out gnats and swallowed camels. Isn't that what we do when we worry about the communion fast and ignore the commands of peace and forgiveness? If there is a falling out among us, should it not occur to us that we need to settle things before we gather as Church the following Sunday? Don't we know that this settling of differences is true worship, as the author of the letter of James would say?

The sign of peace is also, of course, an exchange of the wish of Christ's peace for each other. It is a statement and a desire: *Christ's peace is here; may you experience it.* Christ's peace, not the peace of the world. The world's peace is the peace of good order, of laws and customs being followed. The peace of

151

Christ is in the heart and from the heart, a heart that experiences God's presence and love and forgiveness, a heart that experiences the welcome and forgiveness and love of one's brothers and sisters in the Lord, a heart that is free from greed and lust and unforgiveness, a heart that knows joy in the presence of the Lord and the community, a heart that is enriched by generosity.

After the sign of peace we have the prayer "Lamb of God," during which the presider prays silently. One of the options for this prayer asks that our eating and drinking of the body and blood of Christ may be, not to our condemnation, but to our healing of mind and body.

The earliest images of Eucharist are of the disciples gathering in each other's homes. As I said a little earlier, Paul gives us the first description in I Corinthians 11; and, interestingly enough, he does it while telling the Corinthians that what they were doing was *not* the Lord's supper. He complains that there are opposing groups, that some get drunk, and that some go hungry while others eat. Paul goes on to say, "If anyone eats the Lord's bread or drinks from his cup in a way that dishonors him, he is guilty of sin against the Lord's body and blood. So, then, everyone should examine himself first, and then eat the bread and drink from the cup. For if he does not recognize the meaning of the Lord's body when he eats the bread and drinks from the cup, he brings judgment on himself as he eats and drinks."

This is so far from magical rituals! Paul says that when we gather, if there are divisions and factions, if those who have do not share with those who don't have, then *what we are doing is not the Lord's supper!*

Could it be that what we are doing in some of our parishes is not the Lord's supper and, in fact, is to our condemnation because of factions and failure to care for the poor? The sign of peace grows even more significant.

For Paul, to recognize the meaning of the Lord's body is *conversion to community in Christ*. We are a people in Christ who know what it is to be his disciples together, who know that we are members of each other, who love each other in deed and in truth. This is the reason for the constant, unrelenting exhortations

153

of Peter and Paul, James and John, in their letters: "Be of one mind and one heart."

All of creation comes together in Christ. The divine energy, the divine life, flows in and out of all that is. Jesus uses the image of the vine and the branches. In that divine exchange there is no greater or lesser, no more or less privileged. All distinctions are swallowed up in the Spirit: neither male nor female, neither Greek nor Jew, neither slave nor free.

Rosemary Haughton puts it this way:

> Jesus is present in, through, for (the prepositions falter and scramble) all creation, but more especially in human beings, who are *aware* of their membership of one another through this identifying and liberating bond. This is a bond which is the fundamental statement of how things are, of the basic fact of interdependence at every level—physical, metaphysical and social—yet it is in Christ that this fact becomes a chosen way of life, a thing to be celebrated, the basis of new decisions, new social expectations, new political concepts.
>
> The people, the bread, the body, the giving and receiving of life in the body, through the shared bread: "Take, eat, this is my body — this is my blood": the image is strong as that of the vine, yet complements it. This is the image of community, of people round a table, sharing a meal. But the sharing is explicitly not in any hierarchical order, this is not a medieval banquet hall, graded from his dais to servants' benches. I call you no longer servants, but friends, friends gathered at one table, and these friends are not to try to dominate

each other. They are not to call anyone "father," they are to accept one another as blood kin in a family from which patriarchal structure has been eliminated, because the "Abba" of Jesus is very specifically not a patriarch, and his fatherhood explicitly supercedes patriarchy and renders it obsolete and indeed inimical.

Then, linking together the God-incarnate in Jesus the Christ with the human community, the body of Christ, she describes the women who gathered year after year in a continuing protest against the Pershing II missile base at Greenham Common in the south of England. Haughton writes:

> The fellowship in joy and suffering, the breakdown of categories, the sharing and caring for all alike, recalls the decentralized yet strongly bonded network system of the early Christian experience. Sharing of life, sharing of food, giving thanks, giving love, standing against death and laughing, this is the eucharistic experience, the very body of Christ.

When, in our liturgies, the time of communion arrives, the presider holds up the bread or the bread and the cup and says: "This *is* the Lamb of God, who takes away the sins of the world. Happy are we who are called to this supper." We respond: "Lord, I am not worthy that you should enter under my roof. Just say the word and I shall be healed."

155

As we share the bread and the cup, we profess that this is the body of Christ, this is the blood of Christ.

Sharing in this meal is a renewal of the covenant: "This is the cup of my blood, the blood of the new and everlasting covenant, which shall be shed for you and for all for the forgiveness of sins."

The new covenant is this: God says, *I will be your God and you will be my people. I will be with you and for you and in you. I forgive you your sins. I empower you with my Spirit. I send you into the world to save it, to continue together the Christ-presence, to be a light in the midst of the darkness.*

We do not come to this covenant renewal alone. We come together as God's people, united in one faith, one Spirit, one baptism. We have come to this moment having gathered in his name, having been formed by his word, and after offering praise and thanksgiving. We are a people of the beatitudes who are poor in spirit, who hunger and thirst for justice, peacemakers, meek and pure of heart.

As we eat his flesh and drink his blood, we proclaim our solidarity with him *and* with each other, for this is the body of Christ and *we are the body of Christ*. We eat each other, swallow each other, stomach each other. We proclaim our unity in the Spirit with Christ and with all who are now sharing in this Eucharist and all who have gone before us and all who will come after. This is the communion of saints.

This covenant renewal in this covenant meal is healing. We profess its healing power—the renewal of covenant renews the direction and meaning of our lives. We know, profess and choose to be God's people, to love him with all our hearts, to seek first his kingdom. We know that we are precious in his sight and that we are forgiven. We know that the deepest meaning of our lives is that we have been reborn into Christ to help bring about God's kingdom.

This sharing in the bread and cup is healing because it is the Lord whom we share. We come *expecting* to be healed in mind and body as we eat his body and drink his blood. In fact, we should find it remarkable if we are not healed each time we gather for his word and Eucharist.

This gathering is not a meeting of the Lions Club or a union or a PTA or a political party. It is a gathering of the Church, of God's people, of the people of his promises. God comes to be with us. O we of little faith! If only we believed in the Lord's promises, in the faith we profess, how much more the Lord could do among us!

The communion I have been describing is a far cry from the pre-Vatican II days, when it did not matter whether we went to communion or not. To satisfy our obligation of weekly Mass attendance we only had to be present for the priest's communion. Many did not "go to communion" when they "attended Mass." Again, what was really important was what the priest did. When we did *receive*, it was a matter between Christ and the individual. I recognized the real presence of Christ and welcomed Christ into myself. How much richer the new/old theology! How much more demanding!

Obviously, it makes no sense to gather for Eucharist and not share in the bread and the cup. It is like going to a friend's house for dinner, then sitting at the table and not eating. Eucharist is our covenant meal. To share in that meal is part of why we come.

Two brief notes about the communion rite. First, singing has been recommended during communion. The movement to and from communion has often been called a procession that requires singing. Movement there is, of course, but I think it is stretching things to call it a procession. I am in favor of music, but I would prefer it to be instrumental. That kind of music is part of an environment conducive to our purpose. But I prefer not to be singing. I prefer to be thinking about what I am doing and why. I want my heart to be ready when I share the bread and the cup, and I can't do that if I am busy singing.

A second concern is about silence after communion. What a special times it is! It must be allowed to go on long enough so that its depth and holiness can be experienced. We are in communion with the Lord and with each other. The Lord's presence can be strongly felt if only we let it happen. It is often the deepest experience of what we came for: the experience of God in our midst. I know that music, such as a "meditation" hymn, is allowed; but it is far and away a second best to the silence of communion.

After our shared silence we close with a prayer. Since this is our weekly meeting, appropriate announcements are made to share the business of what we are about. It is a great time to share about community involvement. It is a way of connecting what we do in the gathering with the world we are going back to.

The "dismissal rite" begins with "The Lord is with you." This is the fourth time we hear those words. This time it means

> *The Lord is here. The Lord has been with us. Take him with you as you go forth. Go Forth! Formed by his word, in communion with him and with each other, go forth and be a light, a leaven of the kingdom.*

The weekly gathering is meant to be a source of strength and life so that we can, week by week, go out and build the kingdom. The prayers after communion so often refer to our having been strengthened by this Eucharist, but that strengthening is not magic. Nor is it some secret "spiritual" thing that we are supposed to believe in but never experience. It really doesn't happen if we do not enter fully into the liturgy, if we are not gathered *before the Lord*. Perhaps it would be better to say that *we are strengthened and enlivened to the degree that we do enter in.*

Go in peace to love and serve the Lord.